WHISKEY REBELS

Enjoy!

[signature]

Library of Congress Cataloging-in-Publication Data available upon request.

ISBN: 978-1-950500-46-8

duopress books are available at special discounts when purchased in bulk for sales promotions as well as for fund-raising or educational use. Special editions can be created to specification. Contact us at hello@duopressbooks.com for more information.

Manufactured in China
10 9 8 7 6 5 4 3 2 1
Duo Press LLC.
8 Market Place, Suite 300
Baltimore, MD 21202

Cover: photo by ffphoto/Adobe Stock
Back cover: top, photo by Andrea Behrends; author photo by Ebru Yildiz

Distributed by Workman Publishing Company, Inc.
Published simultaneously in Canada by Thomas Allen & Son Limited.
To order: hello@duopressbooks.com
www.duopressbooks.com
www.workman.com

WHISKEY REBELS

THE DREAMERS, VISIONARIES & BADASSES WHO ARE REVOLUTIONIZING AMERICAN WHISKEY

John McCarthy

dp

duopress

For Alvis

CONTENTS

INTRODUCTION

The emergence of the American craft whiskey movement in the early 21st century reminds me of the Seattle rock music scene's ascent in the early 1990s. Seemingly out of nowhere came a raw sound from the Pacific Northwest that sounded both familiar and fresh at the same time. What became known as grunge was just a bit more polished than punk, but less fussy than the "hair metal" scene that had been in decline since its peak in the '80s. Seattle bands were playing empty dive bars and basements while slowly building a following. Over time, their fan base began to expand, and Los Angeles record companies came courting. Nirvana was the first to sign to a major label, and Soundgarden, Pearl Jam, and Alice in Chains followed soon after. While Kurt Cobain, Chris Cornell, Eddie Vedder, Layne Staley, and their respective groups were doing world tours, the local bands who either didn't score or didn't want a major label deal often remained beloved local "cult" bands who never "sold out." The signed bands amassed a national audience and became brand ambassadors for emerging groups around the country, empowering them to find their own sound and build an audience the grassroots way. Suddenly, eclectic hard rock bands from all around the nation were on the scene and a new chapter in American music was in the books.

The entrepreneurs who shaped the American craft whiskey scene in the early 21st century are like the Seattle bands of the '90s. The most ambitious of these early craft pioneers weren't interested in imitating what the big-box producers in Kentucky, Tennessee, and Indiana were doing. These guys were searching for their own sound. When these bold entrepreneurs first came to market, they met skeptics at every turn—they were routinely

WHISKEY FAMOUS: DURING HIS STRANAHAN'S DAYS, ROB DIETRICH WORKED TO CREATE A NEW CHAPTER IN AMERICAN WHISKEY HISTORY.

savaged by critics, stalled by state regulators, and ignored by distributors. But this scrappy community stood strong, pushed through, and got better. Those who persevered began to see their hard labor pay off. First one, then another American "craft" whiskey was acquired by a large company. Distillers that were local heroes suddenly found a national audience. Some became millionaires. Like rock stars, distillers found themselves on world tours promoting their soon-to-be-famous brands. Others chose not to sell. Most were never asked. Sadly, some have perished. But like the pioneers of the Seattle sound, successful start-up brands like Hudson, FEW, and Stranahan's have inspired hundreds of entrepreneurs from all walks of life to make whiskey.

At first, many predicted that this craft movement was more of a moment, a passing trend riding the coattails of bourbon's renaissance. But this new chapter in American whiskey is here to stay. Today's youth will be met with a much richer tapestry of whiskeys when they first step into a bar than anything older generations encountered. American whiskey is no longer a product of three states; it's a national revolution. This book focuses on several of the pioneers who made this movement happen—but first, a little history.

EMPLOYEES GATHER IN FRONT OF WHAT IS NOW CALLED THE OLD TAYLOR HOUSE, LOCATED AT BUFFALO TRACE DISTILLERY (THEN KNOWN AS OFC DISTILLERY), CIRCA 1879.

UNIDENTIFIED MEN ON THE KENTUCKY RIVER BANK WITH WHAT IS NOW BUFFALO TRACE DISTILLERY IN BACKGROUND, CIRCA 1890

INSIDE THE OFC DISTILLERY, CIRCA 1879

COL. E.H. TAYLOR JR., CIRCA 1900

THE MODERN-DAY
BUFFALO TRACE
DISTILLERY, WHICH
SITS ON THE
KENTUCKY RIVER

➤➤A BRIEF US WHISKEY HISTORY

When Thomas Jefferson abolished the "whiskey tax" in 1802, it kicked off a whiskey boom in the United States rooted in agriculture and tradition. Back then, farmers were often also distillers who converted leftover grains into whiskey, or fruit into eau-de-vie or brandy, to be sold, bartered, or consumed. By mid-century, the whiskey business had transformed into an industrial monster, overrun by shady industrial rectifiers who were far more concerned with profit than quality. In fact, much of the commercial booze at the time was downright hazardous to consume. While cheap rotgut was dominating the market, there were some respectable distillers making quality whiskey. One such distiller was Colonel E.H. Taylor.

After the Civil War, Taylor purchased a mom-and-pop distillery on the banks of the Kentucky River and renamed it the OFC (Old Fire Copper Distillery). Taylor put his heart into transforming his humble distillery into a state-of-the-art facility where he could produce quality whiskey. Always the visionary, he installed pricey copper fermentation tanks, steam-powered column stills, and a steam-heated warehouse in an attempt to speed up the aging process. Taylor was a marketing mastermind, but poor business decisions and a ballooning debt forced him to sell a majority of the company to wholesaler George T. Stagg in 1878. Taylor remained at the distillery as an employee for seven years before cashing out. In the separation deal, Taylor obtained the title to the J. Swigert Taylor Distillery, a small facility in nearby Woodford County that had been purchased by Stagg and Taylor in 1882. The first order of business was to establish E.H. Taylor, Jr. and Sons Co. and rename the distillery "Old Taylor."

During this time, Taylor and like-minded cohort James E. Pepper petitioned the federal government to separate their "honest bourbon" from the "imitation whiskey," as Taylor called it, being pumped out by rectifiers. The result was the Bottled-in-Bond Act of 1897. This act decreed that by federal law, whiskey labeled "Bottled-in-Bond" had to abide by a set of rules called Standards of Identity. These rules were designed to protect consumers by guaranteeing the whiskey labeled as such met the prescribed guidelines. (These regulations were a precursor to the Pure Food and Drug Act of 1906, as well as the Food and Drug Administration.) To incentivize bonded bourbon, the act allowed distilleries to suspend payment of excise tax on maturing whiskey until the juice was bottled.

Bottled-in-Bond Requirements

Whiskey in the bottle is:
- From the same distillery (no blending)
- Made in the same distillation season (spring or fall)
- Aged at least 4 years
- Bottled at 100 proof with nothing other than water added

In 1920, Prohibition kneecapped the legal alcohol industry. It took a few decades after the repeal of the 18th Amendment on December 5, 1933, for the American whiskey trade to return to its days of glory. During World War II, many distilleries used ethanol for fuel rather than for drinking, so at the war's conclusion, whiskey was in short supply. The rye market that spanned the entire mid-Atlantic region never revived (decades later, that is finally changing). With America's entry into the Korean War in 1950, bigger companies like Schenley purposely over-produced to avoid another whiskey shortage. But the conflict didn't have the same impact on the United States as WWII, and when the Korean War ended in 1953, distillers were sitting on a whiskey glut. Bourbon sat in barrels longer, and as these older stocks were released, drinkers developed a taste for extra-aged bourbon. American whiskey rode a new wave of popularity that lasted through the 1960s. By the '70s, however, bourbon and other amber spirits had begun a decades-long freefall, as a shift in trends toward neutral spirits like vodka and rum decimated the industry. Another strong contributing factor to the decline in market share of whiskey was the rise of light beer and its massive advertising campaigns, which drove home the idea that easy drinking equals true refreshment.

Bourbon's slow and laborious ascent back into relevance began in the '80s, when the depressed industry started marketing "high end" bourbon.

Elmer T. Lee, master distiller of William T. Stagg (today's Buffalo Trace), released Blanton's, the first single barrel bourbon, in 1984. The following year, Maker's Mark trademarked the dripping tendrils of their hand-dipped red wax bottles, driving home the home-spun feel of the brand that has always marketed itself as upscale. The next decade saw Jim Beam's Small Batch Collection: Booker's (barrel strength), Baker's (107 proof single barrel), Basil Hayden's (high rye mashbill), and Knob Creek (extra aged).

The Kentucky Department of Tourism and the Kentucky Distillers' Association took a page from California's wine country by founding the Bourbon Trail in 1999 to promote tourism. In the global market, key trade agreements between the United States and the European Union led to zero-for-zero tariff deals on exports including spirits, giving American whiskey competitive legs abroad.

The '90s also saw the emergence of the collectors' single malt scotch market. Pricey whiskeys were marketed toward the American consumer as rare artifacts, manufactured in tiny batches by someone's kilted grandpa next to a picturesque glen. They carry the names of the distilleries where they are produced, and their provenance is both genuine and immensely important to the brands. Meanwhile, the American whiskey industry was watching Scotland closely and following suit. Consumers developed a desire for artisanal, small-batch American whiskey, and entrepreneurs started to question why they couldn't provide it.

➤➤THE EARLY DAYS OF THE CRAFT MOVEMENT

The rise in American bourbon's popularity helped jump-start the craft distilling movement, but it was not the only factor. A groundswell around local and sustainable food helped prime consumers, whose appetites were whet for something fresh in spirits. Meanwhile, the bartending community became obsessed with pre-Prohibition drinks, whose recipes were unearthed by cocktail historians. Craft producers now had the attention of the community, but could they deliver the goods?

Craft beer and microbreweries emerged in an environment where a

handful of large producers made virtually all commercial beer. Six companies—Anheuser-Busch, Miller, G. Heileman, Stroh, Coors, and Pabst—controlled 92 percent of the beer market in 1984. Massive industrial facilities were churning out millions of gallons of serviceable but unexciting brews, whose fans would choose one or the other like Pepsi over Coke. Craft brewers blew up this banal scene with many complex European-style ales and pilsners, sparking a massive resurgence in the microbrew industry. By 2016, there were 5,000 breweries in the United States.

On paper, the microbrew model seemed to apply perfectly to craft spirits. In 2000, 9 or 10 distilleries made almost all of the nearly 35 nationally distributed bourbons and the scant handful of American ryes. But the difference, as many a headstrong entrepreneur would soon learn, was that unlike the watered-down beers coming out of the major breweries, the quality of Kentucky bourbon is world class. No matter how organic the ingredients are or how tiny the handmade batch is, competing with the experience, resources, and support of an established, industrial-sized distillery like Jim Beam or Heaven Hill isn't easy. Distillation is technical, and there are plenty of opportunities to screw it up. For every whiskey maker who was getting it right, there were two out there riddled with flaws. If these small producers were going to seriously compete with the heavy hitters, they needed to know their stuff.

But if craft beer's growth in the past forty years is any predictor of the trajectory of craft spirits, most forecasters like what they see. While the two industries are not apples-to-apples, microbrewing's successes demonstrated a proof of concept that entrepreneurs and lenders could wrap their heads around. Microbrews proved that David could take on Goliath. It didn't hurt that in several states, early craft pioneers like Steve McCarthy of Clear Creek in Portland, Oregon, or Rob Cassell of New Liberty in Philadelphia, did the heavy legislative lifting, allowing the next generation of distillers in the early

What Is Craft?

In my estimation, "craft" can be summed up simply: It's a small producer thing, a word used to describe independent whiskey making. We all agree on this, right? Wrong. After interviewing dozens of whiskey makers, I realized everyone has a different concept of what constitutes craft. It's one of those broad, shape-shifting words open for interpretation that's guaranteed to start an argument among the whiskey geekdom at the slightest provocation. Are you craft if you source product? What if you are acquired by a large corporation? Does size matter, and if so, what determines "too big for craft"? Is Wild Turkey's Jimmy Russell not a craftsman? The answers depend on whom you ask. But most agree that the craft community is built upon a bedrock of two things: innovation and transparency. Making interesting products and being open about how you got there informs the entire community. To keep it simple, this book defines "craft" as it's set forth by the American Craft Spirits Association and its 1,500 members. (But seriously? It's just a small producer thing, man.)

ACSA RULES:

VOLUME: A craft producer, whether they distill their own whiskey or source product, makes under 750,000 gallons annually. This sounds like a lot, and it is. But the craft spirits industry learned from the beer guilds, who a decade back set production requirements too low and lost members as they became successful.

NO IMPOSTERS: Companies must not be more than 50 percent owned by a major producer whose total production exceeds the same volume. In other words, the "big guys" are out.

TRANSPARENCY: All ACSA members make a promise to be "forthcoming regarding the spirit's ingredients, distilling location, aging and bottling process." Tell the truth. Be transparent. Share methods and ideas with the community.

2000s to hit the ground running. But perhaps the most influential pioneer was Fritz Maytag, the godfather of craft brew and craft whiskey.

➤➤THE ORIGINAL CRAFT GANGSTER

Fritz Maytag, heir to the Maytag appliance fortune, was way ahead of his time when he purchased a controlling stake of Anchor Brewing Company in San Francisco in 1965. Fritz revived Anchor Steam Beer from obscurity and is widely considered the founding father of the microbrewing movement that took off in the '80s. Maytag was ahead of his time once again in 1993 when he

Here are more thoughts on what constitutes craft from many of the whiskey rebels featured in this book:

"If you are making a signature, quality product that provides unique, interesting value that's based on experience, I consider that craft. For many years we called ourselves a micro-distillery to stress that we made our own product."
—ANDREW WEBBER (CORSAIR)

"Sourcing whiskey is like lip synching. Craft whiskey is an artist space. When a distiller creates something, their fans want to taste what they have created."
—CHIP TATE (TATE & CO.)

"I will tell you what I do not consider craft: Somebody who hires a team to analyze market data, headhunt a distiller, and develop a marketing strategy before they know what they want to put in the bottle. You might be making whiskey, but to me it isn't craft."
—JARED HIMSTEDT (BALCONES)

"The word that sums up the craft movement is community. We distillers need one another, and anybody making spirit who is willing to contribute to the conversation is what I would consider craft."
—ROB DIETRICH (STRANAHAN'S)

"I don't think there is craft beer anymore. It's all beer. Eventually the term 'craft whiskey' will cease to exist as well. You have small, medium, and larger producers. It's that simple. But we need to call this movement something."
—PAUL HLETKO (FEW)

"In order for whiskey to be craft, critical decisions like cuts and blends need to be made by people, not computers. That is the dividing line. The amount of distillate is not more important than maintaining control over your product."
—RALPH ERENZO (TUTHILLTOWN)

launched Anchor Distilling alongside his brewery in the Potrero Hill section of San Francisco and released his Old Potrero Rye. (Fritz thought the "old" part was funny since his rye was quite young compared to most whiskey.)

It was Maytag's involvement in wine, not beer, that led him to whiskey. In 1969, Maytag purchased an 800-acre parcel of land on Spring Mountain, straddling the Napa and Sonoma county lines in the emerging Northern California wine region. At York Creek, a 125-acre vineyard sitting on the estate, Maytag grew 14 grape varietals for California's finest wineries. The fall harvest of 1991 was a bumper crop for grape production, and Maytag found himself holding 100 tons of grapes he couldn't sell. The plan was to convert his grapes to wine and sell it on the bulk market to recoup losses. But instead of selling all of it, Maytag teamed up with legendary California eau-de-vie distiller Jörg Rupf, who founded St. George Spirits in Alameda, California, in 1982. Rupf ran a few batches of Maytag's wine through his still, and while the project didn't amount to more than a few bottles, Maytag caught the distilling bug. Only he wasn't interested in brandy. He wanted to make whiskey.

When Maytag was planning what would become Anchor Distilling, he had no idea how the industry would react to it. He hadn't forgotten how large beer producers made sport of strangling smaller competitors by lowering prices until the "little guy" couldn't make money and choked out. The pressure also forced smaller producers to cut production costs, which led to cheaper, inferior beer for a higher price. Maytag expected the liquor guys to treat him the same way, but when word of his distillery leaked, nobody seemed to care. In fact, the Distilled Spirits Council (DISCUS), the US trade association representing the distilled spirits industry, graciously granted Maytag access to its library for his research.

The first bottles of Old Potrero Rye came off the line on December 9, 1994. It was the doldrums of whiskey at the time, and sprits were considered dangerous, conjuring images of Mothers Against Drunk Drivers, not quaint distilleries making craft liquid. So the early days were slow going. The local press, who was always thrilled to talk about new breweries, was largely silent about Old Potrero. But eventually, glowing reviews by critics like Jim Murray helped put Anchor Distilling on the map.

Maytag wasn't distilling rye for profit. If anything, he was doing it for publicity. The craft beer explosion was becoming apparent to anyone paying attention, and Maytag was determined to show the world that Anchor was a creative and tradition-focused company that didn't follow trends; it started them.

When Maytag sensed the micro-distillery movement trembling under his feet in 2004, he knew from his brewery experience that a rush of inexperienced players would soon be flooding the game, and this could only mean trouble for the pros. If one of these yahoos blew themselves up, skittish politicians might turn against them, undoing years of hard-fought regulatory advances. If craft distilling was going to become a thing, it needed to come together properly.

Maytag and his nephew, John Dannerbeck, petitioned DISCUS's senior vice president of public affairs, Frank Coleman, to allow small-batch distillers into the fold, but it didn't make sense to the majority of DISCUS voting members to bring these small producers in. After all, it was argued, these small businesses had immediate needs that didn't align with the federal or international concerns of global corporations like Diageo, Brown-Forman, or Pernod Ricard. But Coleman, along with CEO Peter Cressy and senior vice president of government affairs Mark Gorman, shared Maytag's suspicion that craft spirits were poised to take off and saw great value in creating an umbrella for these small producers. Their voting members would need more convincing, however.

While Maytag was attempting to organize the industry through DISCUS, a man named "Buffalo" Bill Owens was also following the craft distilling trend. While DISCUS spent the next three years discussing whether or not they would accept this growing craft movement, Owens created what became the earliest road map to craft distilling: the American Distilling Institute (ADI).

➤➤ AMERICAN DISTILLING INCORPORATED

Prior to founding ADI, Bill Owens led the counterculture lifestyle many envy but few have the guts to pursue. Owens joined the Peace Corps as a young man before hitchhiking around the world and later becoming a celebrated photographer who once sold a collection of his work to Sir Elton John and famously captured the violence that erupted during the infamous 1969 Rolling Stones concert at the Altamont Speedway Free Festival in California.

Years later, Owens launched the country's first brewpub, along with *American Brewer* magazine. Owens published a directory of US breweries and distilleries in the magazine, then spent three months touring virtually all of them in 2003. Along the way, he became convinced that there was a future in craft distilling and decided he would help make it happen. When he returned to San Francisco, Owens marched to the courthouse, filed incorporation papers, and founded the American Distilling Institute, the first major trade association for the craft industry.

ADI wasn't a nonprofit; it was how Bill Owens would make a living. To that end, Owens became a resource for aspiring distillers looking to set up shop. If you were in the market for a six-figure copper still hand-built by the world's finest craftsmen, or a 200-liter, German-made eau-de-vie still for $25,000, Owens was the man who could make that happen.

But Owens's greatest impact on the growing craft industry was the early ADI meetings. This was the only game in town for like-minded distillers to share their challenges, solutions, and ideas. There were few universities or websites where you could learn this stuff—no infrastructure at all. Through ADI, distilleries began to unify and ideas cross-pollinated and spread like wildfire. Contacts were exchanged, and friendships were forged. A community began to form. And as this community grew, it created hope that this craft movement could really become something.

➤➤MAKING HEADWAY AT DISCUS

Back at DISCUS, Peter Cressy, Frank Coleman, and Mark Gorman were explaining to its members that the craft community had something that the giants of the industry did not: strength in numbers. Maximizing firepower on Capitol Hill requires broad representation across as many states as possible. The growing craft community was a potential army of small distillers across the nation. This would be useful in opening markets and achieving

favorable tax decisions for the entire industry. It took almost five years, but in 2010, the Distilled Spirits Council Small Distiller Advisory Group was established with Fritz Maytag as the first chairman. Craft distillers now had a nonprofit organization with a network of lobbyists in 40 states and a team of lawyers ready to assist with tricky things like understanding regulations and staying in compliance.

There was another hidden benefit to the Small Distiller Advisory Group. The United States Department of Agriculture (USDA) Market Access Program (MAP), which Coleman also comanaged, is a program of the USDA dedicated to assisting exporters, like distillers, gain access to foreign markets. Part of the USDA's mission is to promote American agricultural products, especially agricultural goods produced by small- and mid-sized companies. DISCUS, with the support of the USDA, began planning events that allowed small producers to present their American "craft" spirits all over Europe, Asia, and South America. By 2014, what had started as a band of about 50 random small producers became a national industry over 1,000 strong. The DISCUS council agreed to allow an elected advisory "small batch" council. The little guys finally had a seat at the big boy table. When Maytag stepped back from his business, Ted Huber of Starlight Distillery in Indiana succeeded him and became chairman.

➔ACSA

In 2012, ADI subscribers were agitating for change. Members' priorities began to diverge from what Bill Owens was offering as a for-profit organization, and many small companies felt DISCUS was too concerned with its own problems to worry about theirs. They wanted a nonprofit organization that would be solely dedicated to their small business needs. Sixteen distillers attempted to acquire ADI from Bill Owens and shape it into a nonprofit. When negotiations fell through, members voted to organize, pool resources, and become their own trade group: the America Craft Distillers Association (ACDA), established in 2013. Tom Mooney, CEO of Westward distillery, was elected the organization's first president.

At first, like ADI, the group was for distillers only; blenders needed not apply. But some members, like Westward's Christian Krogstad, argued against the segregation. In the end, the group compromised. Blenders who sourced spirits would be permitted to join the club, but only distillers could be voting members. Thus, they changed their name to the American Craft Spirits Association (ACSA) in 2014.

➔EDUCATING AND ADVOCATING

In order to compete in the industry, distillers required two things: a communication support network and representation in Congress.

The community quickly made it a top priority to establish a framework

ROLLING BARRELS
AT TUTHILLTOWN

where members are supported through education in every aspect of the spirits business. Quality craft spirits speak well to the entire industry, but producers making lesser-quality spirits can bring the reputation of the entire industry down. Consumers who gamble on one craft product and get burned are less likely to try another. For this reason, the ACSA is focused on providing resources and teaching community members to make the best possible product.

On the legal side, the ACSA's business is broken into two camps: regulation and legislation. In the United States, alcohol regulation is managed by the Alcohol and Tobacco Tax and Trade Bureau (TTB), a federal government agency dealing with regulation, changes, and collecting taxes. The legislative side of the business, meanwhile, plays out on Capitol Hill. Here, ACSA lobbyists jockey for the attention of members of Congress who can introduce bills into law. In 2017, for instance, the ACSA was championing the Craft Beverage Modernization and Tax Reform Act. Inside the bill was a wish list of things that would help the budding industry flourish. Despite the full force of both ACSA and DISCUS, the Modernization Act was not brought to vote in Congress, but the provision dealing with craft producers' largest concern—federal excise tax relief—was picked up under President Trump's Tax Cuts and Jobs Act.

As the trend in microbreweries and family-run wineries caught on in the '90s, brewers and winemakers successfully petitioned the federal government to change how they were charged excise tax. The relaxed regulations allowed small producers to pay only 20 percent of what the big producers pay. But these rules never applied to spirits, and craft producers who have a similar business model to small wineries and breweries were on the hook for the full excise tax. The tax bill President Trump signed into law in December 2017 reduced the FET for all alcohol producers, regardless of scale, to $2.70 per proof-gallon for the first 100,000 gallons. This put up to $1,100,000 per year into all spirits producers' pockets. This helps many craft companies pay salaries, upgrade equipment, and, in many cases, keep the lights on.

While the ACSA scored a significant victory in securing these tax cuts, new rules came with a two-year "sunset clause," meaning the benefits expired in 2019. DISCUS and ACSA lobbied for a one-year extension, and at the time of writing, they are on Capitol Hill fighting to make FET relief permanent. Until this happens, small businesses and their employees are braced for a brutal financial hit. For producers relying on the current FET to stay afloat, it can mean the difference between life and death for their business.

➺THE WHISKEY REBELS

When I was chatting with Nicole Austin, master distiller at Cascade Hollow (formerly George Dickel), she had this to say about the craft movement: "This movement is still happening. But I look back, and craft has come a long way already." Austin is right. This craft revolution is still happening, and we are witnessing a new chapter in American whiskey history being written. Finally, we are starting to see the unbelievable potential of what American whiskey makers can do once they have the right tools.

The people and the companies featured in the following pages are only a few of the many in this community who have worked together to create a whole new whiskey landscape in the United States—the ones who risked so much because they believed in the potential for craft whiskey, and they believed in themselves. They are the modern Jim Beams, Jack Daniels, and E.H. Taylors. Rooted in innovation and transparency, they fight for fair regulations and compete with industry giants to carve out a place for themselves in the whiskey universe. This book tells their stories.

LET'S TALK ABOUT THE WHISKEY

I've been writing about whiskey for about a decade now, and as much as I adore the beautiful spirits coming out of the hallowed houses of Kentucky, Scotland, and Japan, they don't surprise me. For me, the most exciting part of today's craft whiskey scene is the unbelievable range of flavors and styles. I am truly surprised when I stick my nose in the glass and inhale something unexpected, whether it be ethereal or challenging. This vast new spectrum of flavors and styles in American whiskey is no accident. It's the result of innovation. Craft producers are painfully aware of how difficult it is to compete with the world's finest whiskey houses. The idea that you "can't out-bourbon Kentucky" is almost cliché, but the point remains. Producers know how hard it is to compete head-to-head with classic Kentucky-style bourbon, so many delved into uncharted territory. The result is thousands of different whiskeys made with alternative grains, unique maturation techniques, and nontraditional smokes. Innovation is the bread and butter of the craft movement, and the winner in all this is the customer. Here are a few of the main whiskey styles you'll see throughout the book:

CORN WHISKEY: Corn whiskey must contain at least 80 percent corn, come off the still at less than 160 proof, and be bottled at a minimum of 40% ABV. Unlike bourbon, which must be aged in new charred oak containers, corn whiskey is required to be aged in used or new uncharred oak barrels, if it's aged at all—it doesn't have to be.

NEW WORLD WHISKEY: AMERICAN SINGLE MALT IS AN EMERGING WHISKEY STYLE IN THE UNITED STATES.

2   5-12 (36m)

BOURBON: Most of us know that bourbon is whiskey distilled from a mash of not less than 51 percent corn, backed up with a "flavor grain," like rye or occasionally wheat, and a handful of malted barley. But this standard bourbon mash bill has been completely turned on its head by craft producers experimenting with off-beat recipes, sometimes employing alternative grains, pot verses column distillation, funky fermentation techniques, and unorthodox maturation methods to come up with a whiskey that still qualifies as bourbon but tastes nothing like anything coming out of Kentucky.

THESE ARE THE BASIC RULES FOR WHISKEY TO QUALIFY AS BOURBON. THESE SAME RULES APPLY FOR RYE:

- Bourbon must be produced in the United States (it does not need to be made in Kentucky).
- Distillation may not exceed 160 proof (80% alcohol by volume [ABV]).
- Must be distilled from a fermented mash of not less than 51% corn (or 51% rye if it's a rye whiskey).
- Barrel entry must not exceed 125 proof (62.5% ABV).
- Whiskey must be stored in new charred oak containers.
- Straight bourbon (or rye) must be aged no less than two years.

TENNESSEE WHISKEY: This term is a bit of a technicality, but think of Tennessee whiskey as one that meets the standards for bourbon but requires producers to charcoal filter the distillate prior to aging. This is called the Lincoln County Process. It also must be made in Tennessee.

RYE: It wasn't long ago that people thought Wild Turkey or Rittenhouse were the only American ryes, but when bourbon began blowing up in 2009, the craft community looked to rye as the next shoe to drop. It's no surprise that craft distillers were attracted to a whiskey with an incredible history and the capacity for a wide spectrum of aroma and flavors. Perhaps most enticing of all, it's not bourbon, so maybe it's something the craft community can own. Today, there are hundreds of ryes to explore. According to the Distilled Spirits Council, rye production jumped 1,275 percent to 1.9 million cases between 2009 and 2019.

SINGLE MALT: There is a malt whiskey category in the US whose rules share the same basic framework as bourbon and rye: 51 percent malt, aged in a new charred oak barrel, and so forth. But most craft producers have no interest in "malt whiskey." It's not a category with which the American drinker can identify, and the rules are too damn strict. Single malt scotch is aged in used barrels, for example, and American producers would appreciate the same flexibility. But thanks to our Scottish brethren, "single malt" is something we Americans can wrap our heads around. Dozens of American single malt producers have organized to petition the TTB to recognize the category. But with or without TTB recognition, American single malt is emerging as a mainstream American whiskey category that is here to stay.

AMERICAN WHISKEY: Think of American whiskey as anything that does not fit a designated category. It wasn't long ago that the term was marketing speak for "bottom shelf." But times have changed. Today, American whiskey is a celebration of innovation and style as producers of all shapes and sizes make quality products that do not sit in one category.

CHAPTER 1

TUTHILLTOWN

HOW
RALPH ERENZO
INSPIRED A
GENERATION
OF
DISTILLERS

THE DISTILLERY: Tuthilltown
ESTABLISHED: 2003
LOCATION: Hudson Valley, New York
THE WHISKEYS: Hudson New York Corn Whiskey; Hudson Baby Bourbon; Hudson Single Malt Whiskey; Hudson Four Grain Bourbon; Hudson Manhattan Rye Whiskey; Hudson Maple Cask Rye Whiskey
WHY TUTHILLTOWN MATTERS: Ralph Erenzo is largely responsible for the return of distilling in New York State for the first time since before WWII. It was his hard work that resulted in the passing of the Farm Distillery Act, which gave distillers the right to have a tasting room and gift shop on site in New York and inspired a nation of distillers to organize and advocate for similar acts in their respective states.

➤➤A VISIT TO TUTHILLTOWN SPIRITS DISTILLERY

It was a warm day for mid-January when I rolled into the Tuthilltown Spirits Distillery tucked into the backroads of New York's Hudson Valley. Traffic from Queens was miraculously mild, so I arrived early. I walked the expanse of distillery grounds, stretching about a quarter mile along the Shawangunk Kill, a tributary of New York's Wallkill River. To the east, peeking over the distillery's newly constructed rickhouse and a forest of pines, loomed the rock-faced ridge that brought Hudson Bourbon founder Ralph Erenzo here in 2000.

Erenzo arrived in Gardiner, New York, with no thoughts of building a whiskey empire and inspiring a generation of craft distillers. In fact, he knew jack shit about whiskey. Throughout the '90s, Erenzo's career revolved around competitive rock climbing. He owned an urban climbing facility called Extra Vertical on Manhattan's Upper East Side. When his lease was up in 2001, Erenzo purchased the historic Tuthilltown Gristmill property in Gardiner, a 36-acre stretch of land running adjacent to the Shawangunk Ridge. Erenzo had been climbing here for 30 years, and now he planned to turn the site into his own world-class climbing camp.

RALPH ERENZO
TELLING STORIES
ON HIS PORCH
SHORTLY BEFORE HIS
RETIREMENT FROM
TUTHILLTOWN IN
JANUARY 2020

⇥NOT IN MY BACKYARD

It never dawned on Erenzo that Gardiner locals would have a problem with the camp. But the neighbors arrived in force with their lawyers in tow, launching a legal assault so fierce that it kept Erenzo tangled up in the municipal process for years. To sustain legal fees, Erenzo was forced to sell off most of his property and damn near went broke before finally throwing in the towel. There would be no climbing camp.

Looking for something else to do, Erenzo explored launching a winery, but the idea never sat right. There were 128 wineries in New York in 2003, and none of them had a reputation for fine wine. More importantly, Erenzo knew he didn't care enough about wine to dive in. Winemaking is a labor of love, and he barely drank the stuff.

"What about distilling?" Erenzo began to inquire. Nobody really knew. A little digging revealed there hadn't been a legal distillery operating in New York in 80 years. Erenzo's wheels were turning.

⇥ERENZO FINDS A WAY

The Hudson Valley is studded with around 25 varieties of apples and remains the second-largest apple-producing region in the US. The apples grown in this region are fat and pretty table apples. The ugly ducklings, almost 12 million bushels worth, are crushed for cider or canned for pie filling.

When Erenzo came on the scene, competition from Washington State and China had been pummeling the New York apple market. Farmers were fetching as low as $.06 per pound for cider apples, which accounted for 47% of the average crop—a pittance. Erenzo's calculations revealed that by turning apples into vodka instead of cider, he could raise the value eightfold. Boosting the local farm economy in a struggling market was just the shot-in-the-arm idea that local politicians might support. Could this be something that his litigious neighbors couldn't stop?

The wine industry was nonexistent in New York before being jump-started by the Farm Winery Act of 1976, a piece of legislation signed into law by New York's governor, Hugh Carey. This granted wineries the right to sell their product on their property and permitted gift shops and tasting rooms, which attracted tourism and brought a little cash flow to the region. The new law also dramatically reduced licensing fees, making winemaking and brewing accessible to small producers, but the tax break did not extend to distilleries, whose annual licensing fee was $39,575. This explained the lack of distilling in New York. Then Erenzo discovered that Governor George Pataki had quietly signed a law in 2002 allowing distillers producing under 35,000 gallons to attain a Class-A distillery license for $500. The law had been passed at the behest of John Torgersen, who spearheaded the effort in conjunction with the New York Farm Bureau and the New York Corn Growers Association before life circumstances forced him to abandon his own whiskey-making dreams. Erenzo applied for his permit.

When the request was approved, Erenzo looked around. Here he stood, 75 miles from New York City, on a historic site, armed with a distilling license. Erenzo was officially the first legal distiller in New York in four generations.

➤➤"LET'S BUILD A DISTILLERY"

Brian Lee was an electrical engineer working as a consultant at ESPN in Bristol, Connecticut, when he approached Erenzo to purchase a chunk of the land Erenzo was selling off during his fight with the neighbors over the climbing camp. There was a 240-year-old gristmill on the property that Lee thought he would lease out for a few months, then spend the rest of the year making gourmet cornmeal and flour.

A few days in the creaky old mill was enough for Lee to change his mind. The place was impractical, the work dull, and the margins slim. Lee backed out. But Erenzo needed an engineer to launch his distillery.

The men barely knew each other when Erenzo offered to partner up with Lee. Three days later, Lee replied by email: "OK. Let's build a distillery." Never mind the fact that neither Erenzo nor Lee had ever distilled before. People had been distilling for centuries. How hard could it be?

➤➤THE EARLY DAYS

The partners purchased a 100-gallon pot still after taking a three-day crash course on distilling at the University of Michigan's Engineering Department. This was the totality of Erenzo and Lee's formal training.

They couldn't make whiskey until they had a furnace to heat the mash, so their first product was apple vodka. Then Lee purchased a used five-horsepower propane-fired system and spent six weeks putting it together. When they turned it on, it leaked everywhere. They took it apart and did it again. This time it worked perfectly, but the mess set their bourbon program back another two months.

What's in the Bottle?
Hudson Baby Bourbon

THE VITALS: Non-age-stated, but approximately four years old. Bottled at 92 proof/46% ABV. Mash bill: 90% corn, 10% malted barley. Non-chill-filtered.

PROCESS: Hudson Baby is double pot distilled whiskey aged in barrels sized between 10 and 53 gallons, though today the smaller barrels are slowly being phased out and the previously one- to three-year-old juice is now being released at around four years old.

TASTE: On the nose, Hudson imparts a distinct dose of grain followed by sweet corn and a hint of caramel. The corn carries to the palate where it's met with oak, hints of

While basic Kentucky bourbons are aged at least four years, the first batches of Erenzo and Lee's bourbon barely matured three months in tiny barrels. The stuff—dubbed Hudson Baby Bourbon—tasted beautiful to Erenzo, but he needed an unbiased opinion. He reached out to LeNell Camacho Santa Ana of LeNell's, a famed wine-and-spirits boutique on Van Brunt Street in Red Hook, Brooklyn. LeNell invited Erenzo to her shop for a tasting and purchased 128 bottles—his entire first batch. Erenzo had his first significant sale and his first jolt of credibility.

Erenzo threw himself into marketing Hudson. He flew to Paris, and with the help of a friend who lived in the city, placed Hudson in top bars. Then Erenzo returned to New York bragging to beverage managers that his "craft" bourbon was blowing up in Paris.

The strategy worked. The upstart's occasionally spotty distribution as Tuthilltown struggled to keep up with demand only perpetuated the mystique around this cultish New York "baby" bourbon, even at $45 for a half bottle. Shops were routinely selling out, and the media was sniffing around non-stop.

Then, finally, the people came.

➤ BUILDING AN ARMY

While visitors were welcome at Tuthilltown for distillery tours, Erenzo found that without a gift shop or tasting room, they were ultimately in the way. He was forced to direct tourists to a local liquor store to purchase his bourbon and rye. To Erenzo, this was unacceptable.

Erenzo knew that to battle for the right to have a tasting room, he needed to build an army. To find his general, Erenzo appealed to New York State's Farm Bureau. He stated that the right for his distillery to compete with local wineries would most benefit the bureau's own members since it was from this farm community that Erenzo was purchasing local corn and apples. The bureau agreed and assigned a seasoned lobbyist named Julie Suarez to the case. Suarez was an invaluable resource who provided the roadmap through Albany's red tape.

Navigating the minefield of New York politics required slick maneuvering. Erenzo had to be careful to stay on script while attending meetings in Albany, where he was careful to avoid talk of alcohol, a topic that conjures images of protests by organizations like Mothers Against Drunk Driving (MADD), who are prone to giving lawmakers hell. The message was always about farming, tourism, taxes, and job creation—buzzwords politicians can't resist. When the product did come up, Erenzo was careful to stress that this was an expensive, upscale product—nothing that underaged drinkers would be interested in.

The struggle stretched out two years, but in 2007, the Farm Distillery Act was passed. A significant provision in the new law stated that if distillers used a minimum of 75% New York-grown agricultural materials, they could have a tasting room. This was fine with Erenzo. He had won.

⇥FIGHT FOR YOUR RIGHT TO PARITY

Erenzo wasn't done with Albany. He was hell-bent on fighting for parity of laws between wineries, breweries, and distillers.

For lawmakers to continue listening to him, he needed strength in numbers. By 2008, there were about a dozen spirits companies in New York. Erenzo reached out to all of them. The half dozen or so that showed up gathered on the porch of what Erenzo hoped would soon be Tuthilltown's tasting room. He pitched the group his idea to form a guild, reiterating his argument that for politicians to back change, it had to benefit many. Everyone on the porch stood to profit by the law, and soon the New York Craft Distillers Guild was born. Erenzo and his merry band of distillers continued to travel to Albany, pushing to lift regulations so that New York distilling could compete on the same level as beer and wine.

Over the years, the New York Distillers Guild never let up on changing distilling laws to make the craft accessible and competitive in both New York and on a federal level. Erenzo was a founding member of the American Craft Spirits Association (ACSA), a constituency of small American distillers who successfully lobbied to lower the federal excise tax (FET). In league with the New York Distillers Guild, Erenzo saw through additional amendments, including the right to have a second "satellite" tasting room, the ability to sell at farmers' markets, and the increase of spirit capacity from 35,000 gallons per year to the current cap of 200,000 gallons. Other new freedoms included the ability to sell any New York-labeled alcoholic beverages in tasting rooms, including beer, wine, and cider.

Their latest effort is to obtain parity with breweries and winemakers on both state excise tax and the number of tasting rooms distillers are permitted to own. Special Counsel Tom Donahue at the State Liquor Authority helped craft the modernized New York Alcohol Beverage Control Act that puts the interests of "craft" distillers into law:

"Effective April 19, 2015, the stated purpose of the ABC Law was amended to consider, 'to the extent possible, supporting economic growth, job development, and the state's alcoholic beverage production industries and

5
POINTS OF ADVICE TO UPSTART DISTILLERS

According to Erenzo, the most straightforward part of selling whiskey is making it. Alcohol is the most regulated and taxed industry in the world, so if you are considering starting up a distillery, prepare to hit some potholes along the way. Here is some sage advice from Erenzo, who learned these things the hard way:

1.

Remember that the highest margin sale is the one you make at your tasting room, avoiding the markups of wholesalers and retailers. Own your market—your neighborhood—first and foremost.

2.

Gone are the days when small distillers self-funded. Now that the concept of micro-distilling has been proven, there is available capital from private investors to build a facility capable of volume production. For most, you need to raise money in order to compete.

3.

Make sure the space you choose is adequate for the ultimate size operation you are shooting for. Do not overbuild. Ensure your facility has a sufficient water source and waste removal.

4.

Read and reread the state alcohol control laws that apply to distilleries. Same for local governing and zoning ordinances. Meet with local legislators, building inspectors, and the fire department, and establish a relationship with municipal authorities.

5.

Produce and mature as much whiskey or brandy as you can as soon as you can to begin the maturation period and grow an inventory. If things its tourism and recreation industry; and which promotes the conservation and enhancement of state agricultural lands; provided that such activities do not conflict with the primary regulatory objectives of the [ABC Law].'"

➥HUDSON IS ACQUIRED

Erenzo was enjoying one of those perfect summer days in 2010 when the phone rang. On the line was Lynn Renault, the Innovations Portfolio director at William Grant & Sons, a 200-year-old family-owned business and one of the most respected spirits houses in the world. Grant's whiskey portfolio includes Glenfiddich, Balvenie, Monkey Shoulder, and Grant's Scotch, as well as Tullamore DEW.

Renault told Erenzo that William Grant was looking to add an American craft whiskey to their innovations portfolio and Hudson Baby kept "popping up." Erenzo wasn't surprised to hear this. He knew his little whiskey was sharing shelf space with prestigious labels like Glenfiddich. But he was dumbstruck when she told him Grant was interested in acquiring Tuthilltown.

Simon Hunt, William Grant's USA CEO, pulled into Tuthilltown's unpaved driveway in a long shiny limousine, muddying his shoes a bit as he toured the distillery. Hunt viewed Erenzo and Lee's 250-gallon plastic, open-top fermenters, which were basically garbage cans. There were no agitators and no chill filtration system. The guests were polite, but Erenzo figured they would never hear from them again. Then, a few weeks later, the partners were invited to William Grant's corporate office in New York, where Renault and Hunt formally offered to purchase Tuthilltown.

After six years of building their distillery, Lee and Erenzo were not ready to sell. Erenzo was living in a house on the property with his office right across the way, not to mention the hard-earned, newly minted tasting room. Life was good. They turned William Grant down on Tuthilltown but ultimately agreed to sell the Hudson brand. The partners would continue to produce the bourbon on-site while William Grant assumed sales, marketing, and distribution. The deal marked the first "craft" whiskey acquisition by a major house in modern history. Suddenly this little New York whiskey was plugged into the global distribution network of the sixth-largest whiskey producer in the world.

In 2017 William Grant made another overture to purchase Tuthilltown. Fifteen years into the business, the market had been saturated and competition had grown steep. William Grant was far better equipped to sustain the company at this point. The partners agreed to sell. Brian Lee moved

WHEN ERENZO PURCHASED THE TUTHILLTOWN PROPERTY, THE GRISTMILL WAS STILL BEING USED BY AN ARTISANAL MILLER WHO CRUSHED GRAIN FOR FANCY MATZOH. TODAY THE SPACE HOUSES A BAR AND RESTAURANT.

back to his home state of Minnesota, where he joined the Black Swan Cooperage, while Erenzo signed a three-year deal to stay with Hudson as a founder/brand ambassador.

➻ A GRACEFUL EXIT

Ralph Erenzo retired from William Grant in April 2020 in order to spend time with his son, Gable, who built a small-batch brandy distillery on the outskirts of Gardiner, New York, and a restaurant and tasting room in the center of town that specializes in New York spirits.

But even in retirement, Erenzo's legacy lives on. By the time Tuthilltown pushed the Farm Distillery Act into law, the seeds of the craft distilling community were already being sown: St. George in Alameda, California; Balcones in Waco, Texas; and Westland in Seattle, Washington, were a few distilleries spearheading similar movements. But it was Erenzo who blew the doors open, empowering a generation of distillers to demand changes to archaic laws and sparking a craft distilling revolution along the way.

EXPLORING NEW YORK'S FINEST

When Erenzo opened Tuthilltown in 2003, there were zero operating distillers in New York, a state that had once enjoyed a prolific spirits trade dating back to the 16th century. Today there are over 150 distilleries in all corners of the state, many producing fine whiskeys in guest-friendly distilleries complete with hip cocktail bars and tasting rooms. Here are a few of the best New York producers.

High Peaks Distilling, Lake George

ESTABLISHED: 2016

THE WHISKEYS: Cloudsplitter Straight Single Malt

THE STORY: Opening a micro-distillery in Lake George, a massive recreation area in New York State's Adirondack Mountains, was a natural move for High Peaks founder John Carr, an entrepreneur who had previously launched the Adirondack Brewery in 1999. Carr brings his brewer's background into the distillery by fermenting the wash at his brewery, then head distiller Aaron Koch batch distills malt barley in hybrid copper pot and column stills before it ages for two years in American and European oak casks. The result is Cloudsplitter, an impressive single malt that has been punching well above its weight in the competition circuit.

New York Distilling Company, Brooklyn

ESTABLISHED: 2011

THE WHISKEYS: Mr. Katz's Rock & Rye; Ragtime Rye

THE STORY: Brooklyn Brewery founder Tom Potter, his son Bill, and Allen Katz, former director of Spirits Education & Mixology for Southern Wine & Spirits, joined forces to launch New York Distilling Company in 2011. Katz's infatuation with the emerging New York cocktail scene inspired him to focus on gin and rye whiskey inside the tin-walled Brooklyn-based distillery, once the home of a rag factory. Taking full advantage of the Farm Distillery Act, Katz and the Potters opened The Shanty, a full-service cocktail bar inside the distillery. NYDC's Ragtime Rye is a recipe of 75% rye, cut with almost equal parts corn and malted barley, aged three to six years, and bottled at 90.4 proof, and it is known for its curious tropical fruit flavors.

Cooperstown Distillery, Cooperstown

ESTABLISHED: 2013

THE WHISKEYS: Cooper's Ransom Rye; Cooper's Legacy Bourbon; Cooper's Classic American Whiskey; rum, vodka, and gin

THE STORY: If you love beer, baseball, and bourbon, then a trip to iconic Cooperstown is a perfect getaway. Tour the National Baseball Hall of Fame before hitting the Brewery Ommegang for lunch, then visit the Cooperstown Distillery where you'll likely meet Gene Marra, the entrepreneur who founded the distillery in 2013. Marra opened his first restaurant in Atlanta at 23 years old and then a winery in northern Georgia before relocating to Cooperstown. It was here that Marra decided to marry spirits with baseball. Cooperstown's main jam is Cooper's Legacy Bourbon, which comes in a baseball-shaped glass decanter and was recently described in *Jim Murray's Whisky Bible* as "liquid gold."

Black Button Distilling, Rochester

ESTABLISHED: 2012

THE WHISKEYS: Four Grain Straight Bourbon; Single Barrel Straight Bourbon; Double Barrel Straight Bourbon; Cask Strength Straight Bourbon; Empire Rye; American Straight

THE STORY: Jason Barrett broke a four-generation family tradition when he opted out of a career in the button-making industry to distill whiskey at 24 years old. In 2012, Barrett sold his house and moved back to his hometown of Rochester to launch Black Button, a serious grain-to-glass distillery that is dedicated to supporting the local farm community from which they source their grains. In spring 2018, Barrett opened his own farm—Black Button Farm & Forestry—where the distillery grows juniper for gin and white oak to craft bourbon barrels. Black Button's flagship is its four-grain bourbon, a mash of New York–harvested corn, wheat, malt barley, and rye.

Coppersea Distilling, New Paltz

ESTABLISHED: 2011

THE WHISKEYS: Excelsior Bourbon; Bonticou Crag Straight Malt Rye; Big Angus Green Malt

THE STORY: Coppersea is a farm-to-glass producer of single malt, bourbon, and malted rye, located on a 75-acre working farm in New York's Hudson Valley just a few miles from Tuthilltown. Chief distiller and blender Christopher Williams distills homegrown and local heirloom corn, rye, and barley in old-school direct-fired pot stills. In 2012, Coppersea became the first New York distillery to floor malt its own rye and barley, and Coppersea's Excelsior bourbon is aged in barrels coopered with Hudson Valley–sourced oak. Williams is a founding member of the New York State Distillers Guild and cofounder of the Empire Rye Association, a guild of rye producers dedicated to establishing "Empire Rye" as a protected designation.

GETTING A CRAFT WHISKEY COMPANY OFF THE GROUND

CREATING A MODERN CRAFT WHISKEY COMPANY is a tricky proposition. Whether you are building a mom-and-pop farm operation or a larger-scale start-up, it takes at least three years, depending on how long you choose to age and hundreds of other factors. Distilling requires a continuous infusion of cash to feed your stills and build inventory while waiting years to make back your first penny once your whiskey is aged, bottled, and cleared by the government. Only those with the deepest of pockets can ride this out, and those who try to swing it on a shoestring budget run into cash flow issues, requiring producers to give up equity or take on debt for capital to meet demand. Craft whiskey producers address these financial realities in different ways:

WHITE TO BROWN: Clear or flavored spirits like vodka, rum, liqueurs, or gin can be produced more quickly and cheaply than whiskey. The downside is that every day you are making white spirit is a day you are not laying down barrels, which comes back to you years down the line when you can't fill your orders. Distillers also sell white dog, or moonshine, which is simply unaged whiskey. Many produce white spirits as a "gateway" product until their whiskey is ready, but others have always planned a diverse portfolio of spirits.

RAPID AGING: Whiskey in small 8-, 15-, or 30-gallon oak barrels instead of a standard 53-gallon is a route for craft producers that comes with its own set of pros and cons. The smaller the barrel, the more wood-to-liquid ratio, meaning you pick up flavor more quickly. The challenge is teasing out the tasty flavors and leaving behind woody notes, excessive tannin, and off flavors. Craft producers are a persistent group, though, and instead of abandoning the plan, they've figured out these quality issues. Whether it's better than a traditional maturation, any craft producer will tell you it is up to the consumer to decide.

OFF-THE-SHELF: Sourcing whiskey means purchasing alcohol from another producer with the intention of bottling the liquor under your own label. Most of these whiskeys are made in massive distilleries in Kentucky, Tennessee, or Indiana. On its face, sourcing isn't a bad thing. Blending whiskey is an honorable craft. While Americans deign the "master distiller" king of the whiskey castle, Scotland has always awarded the blender its highest respect. But since blending companies and micro-distillers play in the same sandbox, things become sticky. Craft distillers don't love competing against big box-produced products from established distilleries like Four Roses or Midwest Grain Products (MGP). However, there is mutual respect, and the fact that many producers both source and distill leads most to accept the reality that distillers and blenders need to coexist to keep the community strong.

ALL-OF-THE-ABOVE: There's nothing stopping anybody from having a diverse portfolio of gins and vodkas while sourcing whiskey and aging their own distillate in small barrels and simultaneously laying down large barrels to play the long game. Adaptation and innovation are key in this business. In fact, innovation is what this movement is all about.

CHAPTER 2

WESTWARD

HOW CHRISTIAN KROGSTAD FUELED THE EMERGENCE OF AMERICAN SINGLE MALT

THE DISTILLERY: Westward
ESTABLISHED: 2004
LOCATION: Portland, Oregon
THE WHISKEYS: American Single Malt; Oregon Stout Cask; Cask Strength
WHY WESTWARD MATTERS: Christian Krogstad was a founding member of the American Single Malt Whiskey Commission (ASMWC), a coalition formed to "establish, promote, and protect the category of American Single Malt Whiskey." Today, over 120 producers are currently aging around five million gallons of this American version of a Scotch tradition in all corners of the United States. As liquor conglomerates like Diageo, Rémy Cointreau, and Proximo invest in this space, it seems likely that Krogstad and other producers will see the day when American single malt is as ubiquitous as bourbon or rye.

➠➤WELCOME TO DISTILLERY ROW

I met Christian Krogstad and his wife, Christina, at Flying Fish in Downtown Portland, a no-frills fish market with a lunch counter and a few tables. We broke bread over fresh oysters and Dungeness crab, washed down with local craft brews and a crispy Willamette chardonnay. The casual seafood joint was focused on quality, not pretension, and the choice spoke volumes to what Krogstad, one of the most influential American craft distillers, is all about. Reserved, casual, and true-to-self, this unassuming entrepreneur created Aviation Gin, Krogstad Aquavit, and Westward, an American single malt whiskey.

The Westward Whiskey Distillery is a $6-million facility located inside a warehouse space in southeast Portland's Pearl District. Westward is one of seven distilleries clustered in the area, marketed by the city as "Portland's Distillery Row." Inside the distillery, employees blast punk, grunge, and all manner of metal. Sinks have stickers on them reading "Employees Must Carve SLAYER in Forearms Before Returning to Work." My kind of place.

CHRISTIAN KROGSTAD,
FOUNDER OF WESTWARD
WHISKEY AND INVENTOR
OF AVIATION GIN

The whiskey made at Westward isn't bourbon or rye. This is American single malt—locally malted two-row barley, double pot distilled, and aged in an oak barrel five years. A brewer by trade, Krogstad's obsession with the effects of the fermentation process on malted barley is what drives Westward's style, which is entrenched in the culture of the Pacific Northwest craft brewing scene from which Krogstad hails. While old-school scotch and bourbon whiskeys are bound in their production by laws and traditions, Krogstad has the unfettered latitude to utilize the advances made in brewing science over the past 50 years and apply it to distilling whiskey.

➤➤THE BIRTH OF HOUSE SPIRITS

Christian's name is pronounced *Christ-yan*, as his Scandinavian parents intended. He started home-brewing as a high-schooler in Seattle, one of

CHRISTIAN KROGSTAD EXPLAINS:
Malting and Fermenting Barley Grain

MALTING BARLEY

Malting barley has been a European whiskey-making tradition for half a millennium. There are two reasons for doing so: flavor and fermentation. Malting barley produces enzymes that will convert starch into sugar, and to make alcohol, you need sugar. Here's how it works.

1. STEEPING: Cleaned and sorted barley is submerged in water in a steep tank for about a day and a half, until the seed absorbs enough water that it begins to sprout.

2. GERMINATION: The just-sprouting barley is laid out in a humidity-controlled chamber. In traditional European "floor malting," the grain bed is about a foot deep and is hand-turned to keep rootlets from intertwining. In modern malting, germination beds are about four feet deep, with a screen bottom through which moist air is blown, and mechanical turners are used to separate seeds. In either case, the seed produces the enzymes required to convert starch to sugar. This takes about four days.

3. KILNING: The germinated barley is transferred to the kiln where warm, dry air is blown through the grain to dry it and kill the sprout. The temperature is raised, and the hotter air develops the color and flavor of the malt. Kilning takes about a day.

FERMENTING MALTED BARLEY

1. The malted barley now has the enzymes required to convert starch to the sugar that yeast needs to make alcohol. In the wash stage, the barley malt is crushed in a mill, then combined with 148–160° hot water in the mash tun, also called a cooker. The hot water activates the malt's natural enzymes, converting starches into sugars. This takes 30–60 minutes.

2. The sugar-water solution is strained off and pumped to the kettle, leaving the spent grain behind. This is called lautering.

3. Next, boil the wash to kill bacteria. The sterilized liquid is chilled, then pumped into a fermentation tank.

4. Yeast is added to the wash to begin the fermentation process of converting sugar to alcohol. Yeast is a living unicellular fungus that eats the sugar in the mash and excretes it as alcohol. After four to six days, the yeast goes dormant and the alcohol content is about 8 percent (this varies). Now you have beer. This is what's going into the pot still.

What's in the Bottle? Westward American Single Malt

THE VITALS: 100% malted barley. New white charred #2 oak. Non-age-stated (NAS). ABV: 45% (90 proof). Non-chill-filtered.

PROCESS: All of Westward's whiskey is inspired by both traditional single malt and craft brewing traditions. Two malt barley is sourced from the Pacific Northwest, mainly Washington, Oregon, and Idaho. Wash made from these grains is cold fermented and double pot distilled before aging in standard 53-gallon, number 2 char, white American oak barrels. The whiskey matures about five years in the flat and humid Portland climate that rarely rises higher than 81 degrees or drops below freezing.

TASTE: Malted barley imparts flavors of cereal, malt, chocolate, and spice, while Westward's new oak barrels contribute vanilla, caramel, and herbal notes. But it's the esters from brewer's yeast that define Westward's fruity flavor profile of big citrus and banana flavors.

the first craft brew towns in the early '80s. At 25, he scored his first legit brewing gig at Hillsdale, a McMenamins-owned brewery.

It was 1998 when McMenamins—a legendary, family-owned collection of hotels, theaters, and brewpubs all over Portland—expanded their local beer and wine fiefdom to include whiskey. The company installed a pot still to make a scotch-inspired malted barley at Edgefield Brewery, across town from Hillsdale. Krogstad's buddy and fellow brewer Lee Medoff was named distiller. Krogstad would brew fresh washes of beer and drive tanks to Medoff on a forklift to feed the still. This was his first experience with whiskey, and right away he was hooked. "Shit, I can do that," he told himself. Lee Medoff agreed. In 2004, Medoff and Krogstad quit their jobs, partnered up, and scraped together $65K with credit cards, savings accounts, and equity loans. House Spirits was born.

Their first location was a 1,200-square-foot garage in Corvallis, Oregon, a college town located an hour south of Portland. They got ahold of a tiny 65-gallon, hand-hammered copper pot still and a 200-gallon stainless-steel pot, which was basically a stripping still. They started by purchasing neutral grain spirit from other producers and "rectified" it by redistilling it through their own equipment. This became their first product, House Spirits Vodka. They couldn't afford a mash cooker, so they prepped the malted barley for their whiskey at a friend's brewery, then drove it back to House Spirits to ferment and distill. They called themselves "distillation gypsies." While the whiskey matured, the next step was installing a gin still and experimenting with botanical recipes.

⇒TAKING FLIGHT

When House Spirits began, there were maybe 35 "craft" distilleries in the country, and only a handful of those were making gin. This was 2006, when the craft beer revolution was in full swing. Craft spirits were a natural extension of this movement, so consumers and especially bartenders embraced the idea of something new, something special—something not produced by a big brand. Aviation checked those boxes.

To develop what Krogstad calls an "American Dry," House Spirits partnered with Seattle bartender Ryan Magarian and created a rounder, more botanically balanced gin than the juniper-forward bite of a London dry. At the time, Magarian was consulting on cocktail programs all over the world, hanging out with bartending royalty in New York before jetting off to Europe to do the same. By the time Aviation launched, Magarian had already

introduced the gin to the most influential bartenders in the hottest bars, so it began with built-in street cred right before the cocktail scene exploded.

House Spirits released its first whiskey, House Spirits Oregon Single Malt, in 2009. Around this time, Lee Medoff left to launch Bull Run Distilling Company, a few miles from Westward. Krogstad worked endlessly to keep the company going, hitting festivals, attending sales calls, and managing the distillery. The money coming in was shoveled right back into growing Aviation, and anything left over went toward filling whiskey barrels. Krogstad was going to need some help taking it to the next level.

Tom Mooney had most recently been the chief marketing officer of Fiji Water when he met Krogstad at a trade show in 2010. Mooney had grown up in Guatemala before moving to the states for college, where he earned his MBA at Harvard Business School. He'd been tracking the growing craft spirits trend and felt the time was right to invest, preferably in a growing company with smart leadership and a proven product. Krogstad was in a place where he could use a cash infusion to beef up production, but what he needed most was a partner who was an expert in critical areas like distribution management and fundraising—skills Krogstad lacked. So Mooney and Krogstad joined forces and went about raising capital to lay down more whiskey while grooming Aviation for eventual sale.

Aviation was sold in November 2015 to House Spirits distributor Davos Brands. Actor Ryan Reynolds joined as a partner, and today Aviation is a common sighting on back bars across the world. While Krogstad continues to make the gin at Westward on SE Washington Street, the sale allowed Krogstad and Mooney to reinvest in the distillery and focus on production of their single malt whiskey program. To reflect this focus, they moved away from their original name, House Spirits Distillery, and rebranded as Westward Whiskey, all the while preaching the bible of their American-made single malt.

➦ RISE OF THE AMERICAN SINGLE MALT WHISKEY COMMISSION

In 2012, Krogstad changed Westward's bottles from "Oregon Single Malt" to read "American Single Malt." This trending category was picking up steam as malt barley whiskey producers multiplied. Single malt producers like Balcones in Texas, St. George Spirits in California, and Triple Eight in Massachusetts were popping up all over the United States.

In February 2016, Krogstad and a dozen single malt producers gathered in Binny's, a Chicago liquor store chain, during an American Craft Spirits Association convention at the invitation of Steve Hawley, marketing director at Westland Distillery. Hawley and Westland lead distiller Matt Hofmann made the case that by forming a single malt coalition, they could maximize efforts in establishing American single malt as a legitimate category. This meant lobbying the Alcohol and Tobacco Tax and Trade Bureau (TTB) to recognize American single malt and assign a set of rules that govern how the spirit is made. These rules are called the Standards of Identity. If you submit a legally recognized spirit like bourbon or rye to the TTB for approval and it does not conform to legal bourbon guidelines, it's not going to be released. Besides, if Scotland, Ireland, and Japan all had a recognized single malt category, why not the United States? When a vote was taken, all hands went up. The American Single Malt Whiskey Commission was formed. Small-batch distillers were now unified in streamlining the promotion of American single malt. This collective firepower would educate consumers, create a voice in Washington, and put the whiskey community on notice: Bourbon was no longer the only game in town.

At the time of writing, eight years of persistent lobbying has not been enough to persuade the TTB to adopt American single malt, but the ASMWC has not backed off and the resistance hasn't stopped it from publishing Standards of Identity. There are still no legal protections preventing bad actors from labeling their nonconforming products American single malt, but the power of shame goes a long way. To date, it's hardly been an issue. These producers remain hell-bent on blowing up American single malt whether the government recognizes them or not.

The American Single Malt Whiskey Commission Standards of Identity

This set of "rules" as defined by the American Single Malt Whiskey Commission was designed to be a big-tent approach, allowing distillers to be as creative as possible while maintaining a structure that assures a baseline of quality:

- 100% malted barley
- From a single distillery
- American produced
- Bottled at minimum 40% ABV (80 proof)
- Matured in oak casks smaller than 700 liters
- You can distill up to 160 proof

Compared to scotch or bourbon, the rules are loose. Bourbon requires a new charred oak barrel. Scotch is predominantly aged in used barrels. American single malt allows for both. Double pot distillation is required in Scotland for whisky to qualify as single malt, but American single malt does not specify a still type. Krogstad admits this is mainly because producers in the committee, like FEW, use a column still and the pot-still guys didn't want to kick them out.

SOURCE: *HTTP://WWW.AMERICANSINGLEMALTWHISKEY.ORG*

➤➤THE FUTURE OF AMERICAN SINGLE MALT

When Krogstad began in 2004, nobody expected small-batch malt barley producers to break out of the town in which they distilled, let alone find themselves acquired by major companies. But slowly, this began happening. Stranahan's Colorado whiskey was the first, being purchased by Proximo Spirits in December 2010. Westland was the first whiskey labeled "American single malt" to be acquired when Rémy Cointreau purchased them in 2016. A similar fate likely awaits Westward.

In 2018, Diageo—one of the world's largest spirits and beer producers—entered as a minority owner of Westward through their "spirits accelerator," Distill Ventures. Distill Ventures is essentially a group of talent scouts for the liquor industry whose job is to sleuth out promising craft liquor brands in early development. The company is exclusively funded by Diageo, whose vast portfolio would take pages to list; Johnnie Walker, Bulleit, and Oban are just a few of the whiskeys in their stable. Diageo mapped out pillars for Westward to hit: sales goals, production efficiencies, increased market saturation, things like that. If these goals are met and the relationship remains stable, Diageo will likely purchase a majority stake in the company. Krogstad and Mooney's deal with Diageo stipulates that once Westward is acquired, the partners will remain in their respective roles for a predetermined period. For Krogstad, the partnership is a good fit.

Having companies like Diageo investing in American single malt should be great news for all producers involved. When you have a company with the ability to seriously raise awareness of an emerging category, the exposure they create for one should benefit all. The growth of innovative companies like Westward, backed by muscle from companies like Diageo, makes it not so inconceivable that American single malt will soon earn its perch on the bar shelf, right next to bourbon and rye.

➥WHISKEY IN WINE COUNTRY

Christian Krogstad created a template for success in the craft industry, forging a path for others to follow. He's worked to create a prolific, inclusive distilling community that's rooted in transparency, sharing of knowledge, and building awareness for the movement. Krogstad plans to remain with Westward for the foreseeable future, but what comes next is already in play: Christian and his wife are on the hunt for a little plot of land deep in wine country, Oregon's Willamette Valley. That's where Christian hopes to lead a quiet life distilling what will become Krogstad Family Reserve American Single Malt.

5 AMERICAN SINGLE MALT DISTILLERIES, 5 DIFFERENT STYLES

Westland Distillery, Seattle, Washington

ESTABLISHED: 2010

THE WHISKEYS: American Oak; Peated; Sherry Wood American Single Malt

THE STORY: Local terroir, brewing, and scotch whisky are a few influences that drive the personality of American single malt, and Westland is the result of all three. Distiller and company cofounder Matt Hofmann studied brewing in Scotland before returning to Seattle, where he infuses his talent for beer and love for terroir-driven single malt scotch into every bottle of Westland. Hofmann starts with a wash made from Pacific Northwest grain that's fermented with Belgian Saison brewer's yeast, then double pot distills 100 percent malted barley, just like they do it in Scotland. But the Pacific Northwest grains and water bring forth a whiskey that's nothing like your grandfather's scotch. Westland's aging program employs new American oak, ex-bourbon, and Quercus garryana barrels (garryana is an oak species native to the Pacific Northwest), but Westland relies more on the character of the malt than the influence of the barrel. Westland is also credited as the original architect of the American Single Malt Whiskey Commission. In 2016, the 13,000-square-foot distillery was acquired by Rémy Cointreau, who is already heavily invested in single malt scotch; Islay's Bruichladdich and Port Charlotte also currently reside in Rémy's portfolio.

Clear Creek, Portland, Oregon

ESTABLISHED: 1996

THE WHISKEY: Oregon Single Malt

THE STORY: Long before a craft distilling movement was a glimmer in America's eye, Steve McCarthy quietly released smoky, Islay-scotch-style single malt from his Clear Creek distillery in Portland. Like Ralph Erenzo in New York, McCarthy is known as a pioneer who blazed the trail for distillers like Christian Krogstad to open shop in Oregon. McCarthy's is a one-pass, pot distilled, peated malt barley from Scotland, where it picks up its smoky taste. The distillate is aged three years in local Oregon oak and bottled at 85 proof. McCarthy sold Clear Creek to nearby Hood River Distillers in 2014, but McCarthy's Oregon Single Malt is still available.

St. George Spirits, Alameda, CA

ESTABLISHED: 1982

THE WHISKEYS: St. George Single Malt; Baller Single Malt; Breaking & Entering American Whiskey

THE STORY: St. George Spirits was founded in 1982 by legendary distiller Jörg Rupf, who was among the earliest pioneers of today's craft distilling movement. Rupf focused on fruit liquors like brandy and eau-de-vie made from California-grown pears and raspberries. Lance Winters, a brewer and former nuclear scientist, joined the St. George team in 1996. A year later, the men laid down their first barrels of St. George Single Malt, which they released as a three-year-old whiskey in 2000. While those barrels were at rest, Rupf and Winters founded Hangar One vodka, which they sold to Proximo Spirits in 2010. When Rupf retired shortly after, Winters assumed control of the distillery and went on to expand the whiskey program by adding Baller Single Malt Whiskey in 2016 and Breaking & Entering American Whiskey two years later.

Virginia Distillery Company, Lovingston, Virginia

ESTABLISHED: 2015

THE WHISKEYS: Courage & Conviction; Virginia-Highland Whisky Series

THE STORY: Virginia Distillery Company is nestled in the foothills of Virginia's Blue Ridge Mountains, but its inspiration is deeply rooted in Scotch whisky culture. Late founder Dr. George G. Moore imported Forsyth pot stills and lured legendary Bowmore distillery manager Harry Cockburn to assist in designing the distillery and the late Dr. Jim Swan to develop the recipe. In the spring of 2020, nearly a decade after its inception, the company released Courage & Conviction, a single malt made from American barley spirit aged in bourbon, sherry, and cuvée wine casks. While these stocks were aging, the company launched its whisky program by releasing the Virginia-Highland Whisky series, a blended malt marriage of their American Single Malt and a whisky aged in Scotland, finished in secondary casks at the Virginia distillery.

Santa Fe Spirits, Santa Fe, New Mexico

ESTABLISHED: 2010

THE WHISKEYS: Silver Coyote Pure Malt; Colkegan Mesquite Smoked Single Malt; Apple Brandy Cask; Cask Strength; Sherry Cask

THE STORY: Santa Fe Spirits is the brainchild of architect Colin Keegan, who grew up in England before relocating to New Mexico to build his single malt distillery in 2010. Santa Fe's Colkegan Single Malt is distilled with malted barley that's gently smoked with local mesquite wood to create a nuanced, unique whiskey that has improved dramatically since the first experimental batches. Aging whiskey in this high desert environment 7,000 feet above sea level exposes barrels to dramatic temperature swings, another flavor influencer that's unique to the American Southwest. Keegan has developed a reputation for pushing lawmakers to help the industry thrive.

CHAPTER 3

WHISTLEPIG

HOW A TINY
VERMONT DISTILLERY
HELPED ELEVATE RYE
TO THE
TOP SHELF

THE DISTILLERY: WhistlePig
ESTABLISHED: 2008
LOCATION: Shoreham, Vermont
THE WHISKEYS: 10-Year; 12-Year Old World; 15-Year Estate Oak Rye; 18-Year; Farmstock Rye Special Edition; 6-Year Piggy Back; Boss Hog
WHY WHISTLEPIG MATTERS: By purchasing small batches of mature Canadian rye and turning it into a big-time brand, WhistlePig founders Raj Bhakta and Dave Pickerell helped put high-end rye on the map, all while working toward the creation of a farm-to-table Vermont rye whiskey that could stand shoulder to shoulder with the products of the world's finest distilleries. A decade since its founding, WhistlePig has become the world-class distillery that Bhakta always dreamed of, even if things didn't go down exactly as planned. And the best news? They're just getting started.

⇥ THE OLD WHISTLEPIG

I first visited WhistlePig Farm in 2015 when I accepted an invitation for a press trip to spend a couple of days at the distillery. When I rolled up to the address, the place looked more like somebody's house than a whiskey company, but when I saw a pair of potbellied pigs (the company's mascot) rooting around across the road, I knew I had found the place. A slightly confused housekeeper let me into the residence, where I waited until the company founder, Raj Bhakta, rolled in, looking, let's say, perhaps "overserved" the night before. As we were chatting, it dawned on me that I would be the only guest that weekend. I suspect they forgot I was coming. This was WhistlePig in 2015. Things have changed.

Raj Bhakta is an entrepreneur and, to put it mildly, a bit of a character. Born of affluence, Bhakta attended private school in the Philly area before studying at Boston College and then playing his hand in finance and a few entrepreneurial pursuits. In 2004, Raj landed a slot on Donald Trump's *The Apprentice*. Raj was "fired" by The Donald on an early episode.

After *The Apprentice,* Bhakta sought to parlay his slice of notoriety from the show into a congressional run in Pennsylvania. What Bhakta lacked in political experience the young Republican made up for in self-promotion. Like President Trump, Bhakta made border control a key campaign issue. To drum up publicity, Bhakta flew to Brownsville, Texas, where he rented elephants to ride across the Rio Grande into Mexico, accompanied by a mariachi band. Bhakta and the group made noise and splashed around on elephants for over an hour before US Border Patrol called the Department of Agriculture, who seized the elephants, sprayed them for ticks, and shut the whole stunt down. Bhakta never made it across the border, nor did he win the election.

Bhakta bummed around India for a while before returning to the States to look for his next venture. While visiting friends in Shoreham, Vermont, he learned that the farm adjacent to his friends' property was for sale. He purchased the 500-acre farm without much of a plan.

Meanwhile, Bhakta became aware of the craft distilling scene and began kicking around the idea of investing in a spirits company. He visited Ralph Erenzo and made an overture to invest in Tuthilltown, but Erenzo wasn't interested. Then, in 2008, Bhakta was introduced to Dave Pickerell, a freelance distilling consultant, the former master distiller of Maker's Mark, and a guy with his finger on the whiskey scene's pulse.

➤→DAVE PICKERELL

If craft distilling needed an iconic image that personified the movement, a silhouette of Dave Pickerell would be the obvious choice. Standing over six feet tall, with a round belly, signature Stetson hat, and jolly smile, Pickerell was larger than life and lit up any room he was in. When this natural-born storyteller spoke about whiskey, people fell in love with the craft. Raj Bhakta was no exception.

Pickerell played football and studied chemistry at West Point as a young man before pursuing a military career that landed him in Fort Knox, Kentucky. There he met his wife and enrolled in Kentucky University to study chemical engineering. Eventually, Pickerell scored a job with an engineering consulting firm in the alcohol industry. In 1994, Pickerell was dispatched to work with the team at Maker's Mark, where he was hired as master distiller and remained for the next 14 years. Pickerell left the distillery in 2008 and opened a consulting business of his own just as the craft distilling indus-

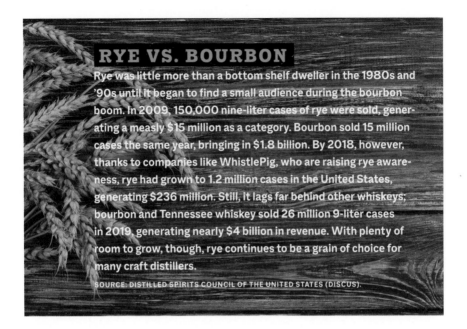

RYE VS. BOURBON

Rye was little more than a bottom shelf dweller in the 1980s and '90s until it began to find a small audience during the bourbon boom. In 2009, 150,000 nine-liter cases of rye were sold, generating a measly $15 million as a category. Bourbon sold 15 million cases the same year, bringing in $1.8 billion. By 2018, however, thanks to companies like WhistlePig, who are raising rye awareness, rye had grown to 1.2 million cases in the United States, generating $236 million. Still, it lags far behind other whiskeys; bourbon and Tennessee whiskey sold 26 million 9-liter cases in 2019, generating nearly $4 billion in revenue. With plenty of room to grow, though, rye continues to be a grain of choice for many craft distillers.

SOURCE: DISTILLED SPIRITS COUNCIL OF THE UNITED STATES (DISCUS).

try was bubbling up. Upstart producers needed all manner of help from an experienced distiller, and Pickerell's phone never stopped ringing. His first client was Hillrock Estate in New York's Hudson Valley.

Meanwhile, Pickerell was shopping around the idea of launching a rye company. Through his connections at Beam Suntory (which owns Maker's Mark), Pickerell had access to stocks of Canadian rye whiskey, distilled by Alberta Distillers Limited, which is also owned by Beam. The rye was affordable, somewhat plentiful, and undeniably delicious. Bourbon was on the upswing at the time, but almost nobody was drinking rye, especially premium stuff like this. But Pickerell believed this whiskey would be a smash once he persuaded people to try it. Anybody who knew him would drink whatever he was pouring.

All Pickerell needed was somebody to write the check. Bhakta was that guy.

➤➤SOME PIG

Bhakta was looking for opportunities in the spirits game, Pickerell had access to this tasty, well-aged rye, and a deal was struck. The guys flew to Canada, where they connected with Jeff Kozak, the ADL sales executive who brokered the deal. Kozak walked Bhakta through a tasting before the three of them hit the town for a great night. Before heading back to Vermont, Bhakta purchased about $200,000 worth of 10-plus-year-old Canadian rye from ADL. The whiskey was shipped to the Vermont farm for blending and bottling. WhistlePig was born.

Launched in 2009, WhistlePig 10-Year Rye was priced aggressively at $70 and quickly sold out. Pickerell's prediction that drinkers would embrace rye was proving correct, and those individual whiskey purchases from ADL turned into a multiyear contract. As demand increased, Pickerell branched out, sourcing stock from other whiskey houses both in the United States and Canada, then blending them into WhistlePig back at the farm. Pickerell began creating a library of endless combinations of rye whiskeys.

The next step was establishing a barrel program where the aged whiskey would be finished in secondary flavoring casks, such as dessert wine, rum, Spanish sherry, dry vermouth, local beer, and cognac. (Mature whiskey is "finished"—meaning aged in a second barrel of various types—for an arbitrary amount of time assigned by the maker. A baseline is about three months.)

This tinkering with flavors led to the first two line extensions: Boss Hog and Old World. Boss Hog is a small-batch, spare-no-expense, limited bottling of extra-aged rye, bottled (and priced) at cask strength and released as a one-and-done limited edition, so it's never the same whiskey twice. It was bold to price a rye whiskey high enough to make a rare scotch blush, but the strategy worked.

To create Old World, Pickerell's team crowdsourced to discover a consensus on a favorite expression. They conducted side-by-side tastings with hundreds of bartenders, beverage managers, and distributors. The feedback was collected and data charted, and to their frustration, the results were all over the map. The experiment failed to identify a winning blend. What landed in the bottle is a blend of Madeira, Sauterne, and port-finished rye, a mix that was struck upon by an intern back at the farm during a group tasting session. From there, Pickerell and his son, Micah, took this combo and perfected it into the Old World recipe. The first bottling was released in 2015.

➤➤BUILDING THE DISTILLERY

For Bhakta, the blending program was the perfect gateway into the spirits business, but he had higher aspirations for WhistlePig. The vision was to create a rye whiskey distillery in Vermont that would rival a prestigious

What's in the Bottle?
WhistlePig 10-Year Straight Rye

THE VITALS: Average weighted mash bill: 94% rye, 6% malted barley (uses various mash bills; the weighted recipe is always 94% rye minimum); new charred oak #3; age stated 10 years; 50% ABV (100 proof).

PROCESS: WhistlePig 10 is a double-distilled combination of column- and pot-distilled whiskey sourced from various distilleries across North America to a batch strength of under 160 proof. The whiskey is matured in #3 char new American oak, spending time in various climates. Some casks spend five or more years in dry, hot Calgary, Alberta, followed by another five in cold, wet Vermont. Barrels of various ages and flavor profiles—be it sweeter, softer, bolder, or spicier—are married together to craft the expression that goes into each bottle of WhistlePig 10.

TASTE: Allspice, orange peel, anise, char, and caramel on the nose. Look for classic rye spice, caramel and vanilla sweetness, and tons of baking spices like nutmeg, clove, and cinnamon. A beautiful viscosity makes this 100-proof whiskey go down smoothly.

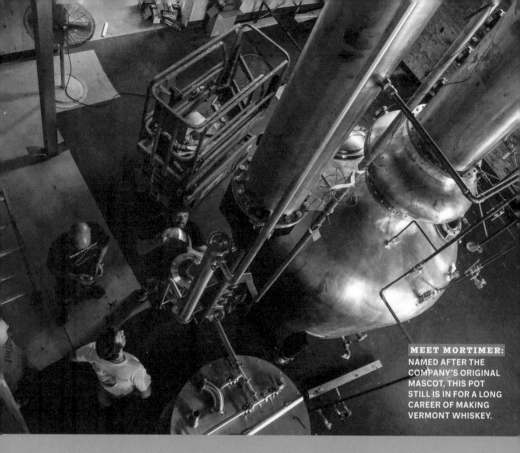

Did You Say Heads, Hearts & Tails?

When distillate comes off the still it contains hundreds of chemical compounds along with ethanol, the flavorless alcohol that we drink. Some of these compounds, or congeners, contribute flavor and character, while others are unpleasant tasting or downright poisonous. These unsavory congeners are present at the beginning (heads) and end (tails) of a run. To find the sweet spot, the distiller will remove the heads, save the heart, then remove the tails. Here's how it works:

HEADS: The first distillate off the still is high in nasty alcohols and other headache-inducing compounds like ethyl acetate, amyl alcohol, and especially methanol, the stuff that blinds you. WhistlePig discards head cuts. Others redistill them.

HEARTS: This is the stuff that goes into the barrel. After running off the heads, the distiller saves the tasty flavors extracted from the grain recipe, yeast, and fermentation. Congeners like furfural (sweet, nutty, maple), ethyl lactate (fruits and berries), and 4-methyl guaiacol (spices, leather, clove) are a few common flavors found in rye.

TAILS: The heart cut is winding down when your proof begins to plummet, since most of the water that ends up in the distillate comes in at the end, along with some unsavory congeners (think cooked cabbages). These are either redistilled or discarded.

distillery in Scotland, like The Macallan or The Dalmore. To get there, Bhakta was going to need more money. Jeff Kozak, the original sales executive at ADL, became instrumental in raising capital to begin construction.

It turned out that finding financial backing was the easiest part of building the distillery. The 150-year-old barn slated to become the stillhouse needed serious renovations: structural reinforcements, a raised ceiling, a new floor, a water waste system, and a septic tank were a few necessities. Outside, they needed a well dug and a filtration system installed for their water source. The entire project took three years, but the biggest obstacle was the state of Vermont—it took five years to obtain the permits required to build.

The year 2014 was stressful for the company, still grinding away at ramping up production and growing inventory while battling the state for the green light to move forward on the distillery. But things got a lot better when Kozak joined WhistlePig full-time as chief financial officer. The most challenging part of this industry is tapping into the distribution pipeline—product flowing out, cash flowing in—and this was Kozak's strength. The following year would be momentous for WhistlePig.

➤➤VERMONT EVERYTHING

In preparation for distilling grain-to-glass Vermont whiskey, Bhakta had invested in growing grains on the 500 acres of tilled land at WhistlePig in 2011. It took a few years to rejuvenate the field and get the rye ready, but by 2015 when the still came in, they were prepared.

To mature their farm-distilled rye, WhistlePig purchases 10-foot bolts of Vermont-grown white oak tree trunks from a logging company. This wood is then shipped to Independent Stave Company, a cooperage in Missouri. To make the barrel, they season the wood by letting it dry outdoors for at least a year before cutting it into staves. These barrels are then coopered, toasted, and charred before returning to the farm as barrels. (The distillery was still under construction when the first barrels arrived, so there was no Vermont rye with which to fill them. Instead, they finished extra-aged rye in the local oak barrels. These initial experiments became WhistlePig 15-Year, released in 2015.)

➤➤A NEW CHAPTER FOR WHISTLEPIG

Pete Lynch was fresh out of college when he was hired as a distiller at WhistlePig in 2015. After a two-day crash course with Pickerell, Lynch stood

next to distillery manager Ben Rowe, who had been hired only two weeks prior, and stared apprehensively at Mortimer, WhistlePig's 800-gallon pot still. Rowe had only slightly more distilling experience than Lynch, and these guys were essentially on their own to make the whiskey. Every step in the process—the recipe, fermentation, heads-and-tails cuts—required testing and refinement, and predictably, mistakes were made. It took time for Lynch, Rowe, and Mortimer to get along, but after six years of preparation, WhistlePig finally began saving Vermont rye in barrels.

Lynch's hiring marked a new era for WhistlePig, which beefed up its young and motivated sales team, many of whom started as interns on the farm. These kids would travel with Dave Pickerell, educating buyers, distributors, and the drinking public about rye. On the farm, a team was developing around Lynch, who was assuming increasing responsibility as he flourished in his role. This team included fermentation expert Chris Dichard, who kick-started the company's indigenous yeast program, which is in line with the company's commitment to Vermont terroir.

This infusion of youthful energy was palpable throughout the brand, which was finally able to release that much-anticipated Vermont rye

into the marketplace. The first drops of youthful, snappy whiskey were blended with mature, sourced WhistlePig stock, then released as Farm-Stock I in 2017.

Pete Lynch was promoted to master blender the same year. In his new role, he began curating a massive library of whiskey combinations. Here's how it worked: Expressions were developed by Lynch at the barn. Employees doubled as a test panel, who were required to weigh in on samples before they went to Pickerell, who, along with Bhakta and Kozak made the final call. Lynch's other responsibility as master blender was hitting the road with Dave Pickerell to show face with distributors and significant accounts. After almost two years of frequent travel, the guys became friends who found sport in ditching the sales crew in any given city to duck into Pickerell's favorite bars, where he'd be treated like a rock star.

⇥EXIT: RAJ BHAKTA

WhistlePig was flourishing in the years leading up to 2018, but Bhakta's relationship with his investors was going south. Bhakta's frustrations with the direction of the company itself began to bubble over, and the board felt like it had a great whiskey company despite Bhakta, not because of him. Things came to a head when Bhakta caught wind of a secret shareholders' meeting held in his absence. Bhakta crashed the party and drama ensued. The fallout resulted in accusations and airing of dirty laundry on both sides, leaving a team of attorneys to sort out the mess. In January 2018, Bhakta accepted a settlement to leave WhistlePig, the company he founded.

⇥A SAD DAY IN CRAFT DISTILLING

On November 1, 2018, the distilling world was stunned to learn that WhistlePig cofounder Dave Pickerell had unexpectedly passed away at the age of 62. He died of natural causes while in San Francisco for Whiskey Fest, a consumer event he was attending on behalf of WhistlePig. His final WhistlePig project was working with Lynch to develop Piggy-Back, a lower-priced 6-year-old rye designed as a cocktail vehicle for the bartending community that Pickerell admired. His departure was a sad day in the distilling community as he left behind his wife, Jeannette, four children, and three grandkids.

But he will not be forgotten. Pickerell's legacy lives on in WhistlePig, which grew from a 30,000-case-per-year brand into what's closing in on a 100,000-case success story. The WhistlePig team has grown from 40 to over 100 employees and continues to shape a whiskey program that's routed in innovation, transparency, and connecting with its fans. The original creators of WhistlePig may be gone, but what remains is a young, vibrant whiskey house that is set up to become the Vermont whiskey empire that Raj Bhakta envisioned back in 2008.

BACK IN THE DAY, EVERYBODY WAS DRINKING WHAT PICKERELL WAS POURING.

PICKERELL
GOT AROUND

Dave Pickerell has been called the Johnny Appleseed of distilling, and it's easy to see why. Here are just a handful of the fine companies Pickerell helped jump-start.

Hillrock Estate Distillery, Ancram, NY

ESTABLISHED: 2012

THE WHISKEYS: Hillrock Solera Bourbon; Estate Single Malt; Double Cask Rye

THE STORY: Jeffery Baker and his wife, Cathy Franklin, founded this pristine farm-to-glass distillery and malt house in New York's Hudson Valley. Hillrock is about as local and sustainable as a distillery can be—all grains are either grown on-site or purchased from a neighbor. Dave Pickerell was with the company from the earliest days, helping design the facilities as well as the whiskey program, which boasts a "twice-casked" rye (meaning it's aged in both medium and heavily charred barrels) and an American single malt that's floor-malted and gently smoked on-site. Hillrock's signature whiskey is their Solera Aged Bourbon, made from a high-rye recipe cut with water sourced from a local stream and finished in 20-year-old oloroso sherry casks before being bottled at 86.6 proof.

Nelson's Green Brier Distillery, Nashville, TN

ESTABLISHED: 2012

THE WHISKEYS: Belle Meade Bourbon; Belle Meade Reserve; Nelson's Green Brier Tennessee Whiskey; Belle Meade Single Barrel Bourbon; Belle Meade Bourbon Finished in XO Cognac Cask; Belle Meade Bourbon Madeira Cask Finish; Belle Meade Bourbon Sherry Cask Finish

THE STORY: The original Nelson's Green Brier Distillery in Greenbrier, Tennessee, was founded by Charles Nelson and operated from 1860 until 1909. Great-grandchildren Charlie and Andy Nelson resurrected the brand over a century later, starting with a blending house in 2012. Dave Pickerell assisted the Nelsons in developing Belle Meade, an MGP-sourced bourbon, and in the planning and construction of an expansive 50,000-square-foot facility inside a historic automotive factory near downtown Nashville. The distillery opened in 2014. Nelson's long-awaited flagship spirit, Green Brier Tennessee Whiskey, was released in 2020. It's a wheated bourbon recipe of corn, wheat, and malt barley, aged two to five years, bottled at 91 proof, and filtered through sugar-maple charcoal. In 2019, Green Brier was purchased by Constellation Brands and is expected to be rolled out nationally in 2022.

Traverse City Whiskey, Traverse City, MI

ESTABLISHED: 2012

THE WHISKEYS: XXX Straight Bourbon; American Cherry Edition; Barrel Proof Bourbon; North Coast Rye; Port Barrel Finish

THE STORY: Chris Frederickson and two of his Michigan State college buddies dreamed up Traverse City Whiskey in 2011. The crew hired Dave Pickerell to set up the team with a sourced whiskey program while they converted a former power station in downtown Traverse City into a stillhouse and craft cocktail bar. In 2014, the crew added a 13,000-square-foot location for production and barrel storage. Traverse City's whiskey program features a straight bourbon and their spicy/buttery North Coast Rye. Since Michigan is considered the cherry capital of the world, it's no surprise that their Montmorency sour cherry–infused bourbon (American Cherry Edition) is the best-selling craft spirit in the state. These days, the company is upgrading to a 35,000-square-foot facility inside an old cherry production plant on a farm outside of town, so expect a lot of whiskey coming out of Michigan in the coming years.

Woodinville Whiskey Co., Woodinville, WA

ESTABLISHED: 2010
THE WHISKEYS: Straight Bourbon; Straight 100% Rye; Double Barrel Whiskey; Straight Bourbon Finished in Port Casks
THE STORY: Childhood friends Orlin Sorensen and Brett Carlile launched Woodinville in 2010 after Washington laws were changed to allow distilleries to sell products made on-site. Woodinville is nestled in the heart of Washington's wine country, with over 120 licensed wineries in a 5-mile radius of the distillery. If you are wondering why someone would make whiskey in wine country, consider that the town of Woodinville attracts over 350,000 visitors a year, ensuring a steady stream of foot traffic that kept Woodinville afloat while they were developing their national strategy. Unlike most start-ups, Woodinville resisted the temptation to source or rely exclusively on small barrels for aging. Instead, the partners played the long game by aging standard 53-gallon barrels for at least five years before rolling out their signature bourbon in 2015. Their rye came out a year later. Patience paid off in 2017 when the company was acquired by Moet Hennessy, who is currently expanding their operation.

Ragged Branch, Charlottesville, VA

ESTABLISHED: 2014
THE WHISKEYS: Virginia Straight Bourbon; Wheated Bourbon; Double Oaked Wheated Bourbon; Double Oaked Bourbon, Bottled-in-Bond
THE STORY: Alex Toomey and his partners knew nothing about making bourbon when they resolved to build a distillery on Toomey's farm in Charlottesville in 2009, so they hired Dave Pickerell to teach them. Pickerell handled all whiskey operations, from ordering equipment to barreling the final product at this farm-to-glass distillery. Ragged Branch is strictly a bourbon house and still employs the exact same grain recipe and product lineup of traditional and wheated bourbons that Pickerell developed for them back in 2014. Toomey personally grows all the grain, rye, and wheat in the mash, and all of Ragged Branch's juice is aged on the farm and bottled at around five years old. The Ragged Branch Barrel Select Program allows superfans to purchase a full barrel of one of five recipes, which yields about 275 0.750 liter bottles.

CHAPTER 4

STRANAHAN'S

HOW JESS GRABER AND ROB DIETRICH BUILT A GRASSROOTS WHISKEY COMMUNITY INTO A COLORADO WHISKEY EMPIRE

THE DISTILLERY: Stranahan's
ESTABLISHED: 2004
LOCATION: Denver, Colorado
THE WHISKEYS: Colorado Whiskey; Diamond Peak; Sherry Cask; Mountain Angel; Blue Peak; Snowflake
WHY STRANAHAN'S MATTERS: When Stranahan's arrived on the craft distilling scene in 2004, it became the first distillery to make legal spirits in Colorado in almost a century. Cofounder Jess Graber was a backyard moonshiner who managed to turn a hobby into a beacon for the community, which rallied around this beloved whiskey company. Graber hired Rob Dietrich, who spent a decade developing Stranahan's whiskey program and fostering the grassroots movement that would morph into a cult following. It was Stranahan's that proved fame doesn't depend on a massive advertising budget. Sometimes it just takes a village.

➤➤AMERICAN WHISKEY

It was December 2019 when I first sat down with Stranahan's former master distiller, Rob Dietrich. We met at American Whiskey, a bar on West 29th Street three blocks south of Madison Square Garden in New York City. Dietrich was easy enough to spot, wearing a leather jacket over a snap-button-down denim shirt and a wide brim hat that sat somewhere between pool shark and Colorado cowboy. The look was accentuated by a bold set of mutton chops, eluding to a rock-and-roll edge honed over a decade in the music industry.

Dietrich was in town for a media tour to promote Blackened, a bourbon from Sweet Amber Distilling, the whiskey company launched by the iconic metal band Metallica. Joining Blackened was not an easy decision for Dietrich. First, the job required filling the role of Dave Pickerell, a friend of Dietrich's and a giant in the industry who sadly passed away in 2018. Also, Dietrich had spent 12 years at Stranahan's climbing his way from the bottling line to head distiller. Leaving a comfortable gig at a successful brand with plenty of room to grow might seem like an unnecessary risk, but once you understand what makes Dietrich tick, you know why the move to Sweet Amber made sense.

ROB DIETRICH
HOLDING COURT AND
POURING DRAMS AT
STRANAHAN'S BAR
AND TASTING ROOM

⇢NEVER SAW THIS ONE COMING

Long before whiskey, Dietrich spent a decade working as a stage manager, lighting technician, and backline manager for bands he grew up idolizing. One night he'd be setting up Greg Allman's keyboards in San Francisco and the next he was sitting in a prayer circle with James Brown. Between gigs, he serviced walk-in coolers for breweries and restaurants in his home city of Denver. Dietrich has always been handy—the self-proclaimed gear head drove a Czech motorcycle called a Jawa that was retrofitted with a diesel cement mixer engine modified to run on cooking oil. Drinking in a nearby watering hole one night, Dietrich struck up a conversation with Jake Norris, a fellow enthusiast who powered his own bike with spent distillate produced at Stranahan's, where he worked as a distiller. By night's end, Norris invited Dietrich to the distillery to check out the operation.

It was love at first sight when Dietrich first laid eyes on Stranahan's gleaming 800-gallon copper pot still. At that moment, he knew he needed to understand everything about this curious vessel. Norris beamed with pride as he walked Dietrich through the distillery, spouting knowledge about the whiskey-making process. The tour concluded at the bottling line, an essential step in production with which Dietrich would later become exceedingly familiar. When Dietrich was introduced to Stranahan's cofounder, Jess Graber, he had no clue he was shaking hands with the man who would alter the course of his life. For the next year, Dietrich volunteered his time on that bottling line in exchange for learning every facet of the distillery. Eventually, they hired him at $10 an hour.

⇢THE BIRTH OF STRANAHAN'S

Before Jess Graber cofounded Stranahan's, he owned a construction company and served as a volunteer fireman in his hometown of Woody Creek, located 200 miles west of Denver. Graber enjoyed dabbling in home distilling in his spare time, cranking "corn squeezins" out of a beat-up 13-gallon pot still gifted to him by a dude named Larry the River Rat in 1972.

In 1998, Graber was called to a barn fire at Flying Dog Ranch, which belonged to George Stranahan, a noted physicist and entrepreneur who had cofounded Flying Dog—a Denver brewpub that evolved into a 100,000-case, nationally distributed craft brew—in 1990. Stranahan's barn burned to the ground that night, but the encounter sparked a friendship. Graber told Stranahan about his still, explaining that he

Rob Dietrich Explains
BARREL EXPRESSIONS

BATCH BLENDING: Barrels of whiskey are dumped into a large holding tank, usually made of stainless steel. The distiller or blender adjusts the flavors, generally with differently aged stocks, to achieve a consistent flavor profile.

SINGLE BARREL: The contents of each bottle of whiskey come from an individual cask instead of a dumped batch of multiple barrels. Famous single barrel whiskeys include Elmer T. Lee, Four Roses Single Barrel, and Blanton's Bourbon.

SPECIAL BARREL FINISH: A barrel finish involves transferring the contents of a barrel into a second container, which imparts additional flavors and characteristics. Wine barrels, rum casks, and even tequila barrels are commonly used. Stranahan's Sherry Cask finish is classic Stranahan's single malt aged an additional four to six months in oloroso sherry casks from Spain, which impart a distinct sweetness commonly found in many scotches.

could only use it in warm weather because his horse shed was open and it's cold in the mountains in April. When Stranahan offered the "butcher" room in another barn as a place to distill, Graber moved his moonshine operation to Flying Dog Ranch.

Graber spent six years making small batches of distilled corn mash at Stranahan's, where George's old friend, the late journalist Hunter S. Thompson, would swing by to tipple some white dog while Graber worked the still. Inevitably, Graber began experimenting with distilling Flying Dog beer, and he was blown away by the superior quality. It was better than anything he was getting with his corn mash. When he presented a jar of malty moonshine and pitched the idea of selling the whiskey commercially, Stranahan told him he was nuts. "Like trying to compete with Chevy with a car you built in your garage," he said. Those who know Graber know he's persistent, though, and when he offered to name the whiskey Stranahan's, Stranahan finally agreed to invest.

At the time, there was literally no distilling scene in Colorado. Graber and Stranahan were about to own the state's first legal still since 1920.

➥AN ARMY OF ONE

The first Stranahan's Colorado whiskey was released in 2006 at two years old. The original distillery on Blake Street was right next door to Flying

THE WHISKEY COWBOY: STRANAHAN'S COFOUNDER, JESS GRABER

Dog Brewery. Beer was pumped through a pipe into the distillery, where it was used as whiskey wash. Graber still worked construction during the day and managed the whiskey business every other waking minute.

By the time Rob Dietrich joined, Stranahan's was already growing fast, and Dietrich was soon immersed in every part of the production, from distilling to filling barrels to sweeping the bathroom floor. There were never enough hours in the day to catch up, which gave Dietrich an idea. He approached Jess Graber and pitched his plan to create a night shift, which he would run.

Dietrich was still making $10 an hour while working that graveyard shift, six days a week for four solid years. This was coupled with an 80-mile daily commute that concluded with a barn full of chores—he was living rent-free at his girlfriend's mom's property in exchange for working on their farm. This was a whiskey boot camp, but it was worth it. In the dead of night, the apprentice became a master, honing his skills, training his palate, and developing the blending chops that would define his career.

What's in the Bottle?
Stranahan's American Single Malt Colorado Whiskey

THE VITALS: 100% malted barley; new charred oak #3; NAS, 47% ABV (94 proof); non-chill-filtered.

PROCESS: Stranahan's signature single malt begins with a variety of barley strains that are malted at the Coors brewery in Golden, Colorado. The mash is fermented brewer's style in closed, temperature-controlled fermenters and cut with El Dorado Springs water, some of the finest in the world. The wash is pot distilled twice, coming off the still at about 140 proof. The white dog enters a #3 char new white oak barrel at 110 proof and matures two to five years in a warehouse kept at 75 degrees and 45 percent humidity.

TASTE: On the nose, there are aromas of black pepper, vanilla, and maple alongside some citrus notes. The palate reveals layers of cinnamon, chocolate, and caramel. The finish begins spicy, then tapers off long and sweet.

⇒→THE WHITE UNICORN

While the kings of the liquor industry battle for market share by wielding massive advertising dollars and employing celebrity spokespeople, Graber threw pizza parties. A zero budget requires creative ways to connect with customers. This is something that Stranahan's has done exceptionally well. These gatherings were (and still are) open to volunteers who worked the bottling line, just like Dietrich did in the earliest days. The compensation was pizza, whiskey, and all the Flying Dog beer you could drink. This grassroots style of community-building was born of necessity, but it ultimately brought local enthusiasts together and directly connected them to the brand, establishing loyalty. The volunteers were encouraged to initial each bottle and leave a note for the customer (Go, Rockies!). While this created buzz around Denver, it was the 2007 release of Stranahan's Snowflake that brought national attention.

Stranahan's Snowflake is a special bottling of a limited-edition whiskey available only at the distillery on one December day each year. In the early years, Snowflakes were single barrel bottlings, yielding about 200 bottles that famously sold out immediately. Each year, fans lined up around the corner and down the block hoping to score a bottle. The first Snowflake was an expression of American single malt finished in a Hungarian white oak barrel. The following year was "Palidise," a whiskey finished in wine casks from Palisade, Colorado's wine region.

Word spread, and Snowflake Day began to feel like a holiday. Devoted fans took to camping outside the distillery overnight, and the next year people showed up three days prior. Twitter and Instagram would light up with photos of proud purchasers showing off their score, and the long lines attracted national news. Over time, this quaint, community whiskey became a white unicorn with a cultish following that began trading for big money on the secondary market.

As demand for Stranahan's in markets like New York, California, and Texas spiked, the company was caught short on inventory. They were ramping up production, but it would take years to age enough stock to keep up. Graber pulled a controversial move by withdrawing Stranahan's from the national market and focused solely on his most loyal following: the people of Colorado. The risky move would either amplify the company's mystique or drive the brand into obscurity. New whiskeys with new stories were launching seemingly every day. How Stranahan's would be received a second time around was anybody's guess.

⇥FLYING DOG FLIES AWAY

Flying Dog moved its operations to Fredericksburg, Maryland, in 2007, and Stranahan closed the Blake Street brewery. With Flying Dog went Stranahan's cost-effective source for whiskey wash. It was time to become self-sufficient, so Graber shopped for a larger facility and landed on the former Heavenly Days Brewery, a rundown shell of a building that was foreclosed on six years prior. There was no power, and the plumbing pipes had long since been stolen. The place had originally been a beef jerky factory that kept adding space as its business grew, resulting in a wonky layout that required creative solutions for effective distilling. On the plus side, the downtown location on Kalamath was perfect and the building had a sweet bar that would serve admirably as a tasting room. Graber mortgaged everything he had to get the lease, and in April 2009, Stranahan's loaded their equipment piece-by-piece onto semitrucks and set up shop.

⇥EVERYTHING CHANGED

In 2010, Jess Graber sold Stranahan's to Proximo Spirits, whose portfolio includes Bushmills Irish Whiskey and Jose Cuervo Tequila. Graber felt the time was right for a larger company to take the wheel, which freed him up to work on new projects, one of which became Tin Cup, an American whiskey developed by Graber and MGP's Greg Metze, who was master distiller at MGP at the time.

Stranahan's became the second craft distillery after Hudson to be acquired and the first American single malt distillery to have the distinction, even though the label read "Colorado Whiskey." Drama ensued during the aftermath, and head distiller Jake Norris resigned. When the dust settled, Dietrich was promoted to head distiller. His first task was to immediately triple production by overseeing the installation of three additional stills and five fermenters. This was the big leagues, he thought, a defining moment that would likely blow up his career one way or another.

Meanwhile, Stranahan's employees were not the only people upset by the sale. The loyal Colorado whiskey community freaked out. Dietrich couldn't believe how many felt betrayed by the sale to Proximo. Loyal followers turned against them, swearing never to drink the stuff again. Bogus rumors swirled that Stranahan's moved distilling operations to New Jersey, where Proximo's corporate headquarters are located. Immediately after the sale, Dietrich received complaints that the whiskey had changed, which was impossible since the juice they were drinking was barreled long before Proximo came into the picture. Dietrich was surprised and a little hurt by the backlash but understood it. Stranahan's was like a club for local fans, and when a big company takes over, it's natural to feel robbed of the homegrown pride that made it special. Dietrich would argue in vain to bar managers that if they stopped carrying products backed by large companies, they'd have to clear their shelves, but he couldn't change the fact that the move broke hearts in Denver.

➤➤REANIMATED

Over time, the sting of the sale began to fade. Fans continued camping out every year to score a Snowflake bottle, and the legendary bottling parties were never wanting for attendees. The transition period from private to corporate ownership was certainly intense, but it solidified Dietrich's career. Suddenly the newly minted master distiller was developing Stranahan's Sherry Cask in the distillery while meeting the press and schmoozing buyers on the road. His rock-and-roll cowboy looks helped make him the face of the brand. The days of minimum wage were gone. The hard work was paying off.

That first year as head distiller, Dietrich transformed the Snowflake program from a single barrel to a full-scale blending program, jumping from 200 bottles to 2,000. His 2011 release was a rum-cask-finished single malt, finished in sherry and Madeira casks. Each Snowflake Eve, Dietrich made it his business to walk the line of the 1,000 whiskey fans lined up for their two bottles of Snowflake. All the picture taking, bottle signing, and whiskey talk might seem like a small gesture, but this level of engagement solidified the brand's reputation. While many people, like Jake Norris and George Stranahan, deserve credit for the company's success, it was Rob Dietrich and his mentor, Jess Graber, who created the mystique that helped put Colorado whiskey on the map.

➤➤NEW SHERIFF IN TOWN

Since Jess Graber left Stranahan's to focus on Tin Cup and Dietrich moved on to work with Metallica, distiller Owen Martin has taken over as head distiller. Martin earned a master's degree at Heriot-Watt University in Edinburgh, Scotland, where he studied brewing and distillation. Working in a whiskey town like Edinburgh inspired Martin to focus on whiskey. After graduation, Martin scored a distilling gig at Rock Town Distillery, where he spent two years learning the craft before joining Stranahan's in 2016. Mar-

STRANAHAN'S, A MILE-HIGH URBAN DISTILLERY IN DOWNTOWN DENVER

tin worked under Dietrich for the next three years before being promoted to head distiller at Dietrich's departure in 2019. Martin inherited two new whiskeys in development: Stranahan's Blue Peak and Mountain Angel. Blue Peak is a solera-style whiskey, while Mountain Angel is an age-stated 10-year-old bottling laid down by Dietrich in 2010.

As for Dietrich, when I caught up with him at Blackened in 2020, he was immersed in experimenting with "black noise sonic enhancement," a maturation technique developed for Blackened by Metallica's sound company and Dave Pickerell, the brand's original whiskey architect. The idea is to blast low-frequency Metallica songs in the rickhouse where Blackened barrels rest. The vibrations agitate the whiskey, whose waves force interaction between the wood and the spirit. Dietrich was setting up control barrels against sonically enhanced barrels to see how the whiskey changes. His worlds of whiskey and music had come together.

DID YOU SAY SOLERA AGING?

Solera, which is Spanish for "on the ground," is a blending and aging system that mingles different whiskeys over time while preserving the DNA of the original liquid. To make Diamond Peak through a solera process, mature single malt is transferred into a 620-gallon new American oak vessel, known as a foeder, for several months. A portion of this liquid is cut to proof and bottled. Meanwhile, new stocks of single malt are added to replenish the vessel, which is never fully emptied. This continuous whiskey development allows for extended finishing times.

EXPLORING ROCKY MOUNTAIN WHISKEY

Nobody was distilling in Colorado before Stranahan's came to town. Now, at the time of writing, the state is home to 400 breweries, 100 wineries, and 80 distilleries, with a brilliant craft whiskey scene filled with passionate producers making great stuff. Here are five standouts.

Leopold Bros., Denver

ESTABLISHED: 2014

THE WHISKEYS: Straight Bourbon; American Small Batch Whiskey; Maryland-Style Rye Whiskey; Michigan Cherry Whiskey; New York Apple Whiskey; Rocky Mountain Blackberry Whiskey; Rocky Mountain Peach Whiskey

THE STORY: Everything about the Leopold Bros. distillery is steeped in transparency, quality ingredients, and traditional methods. After launching a popular microbrewery, distillery, and taproom in Ann Arbor, Michigan, brothers Todd and Scott Leopold moved operations to Colorado in 2005. Here, the brothers built a world-class, zero-waste distillery featuring eight stills of various shapes and sizes, wooden open fermenters, and Colorado's first malting floor and kiln. Leopold's just says no to any industrial methods, including commercial enzymes in their bourbon or rye, opting instead for copious amounts of malted barley in the mash, allowing nature to take its course.

Distillery 291, Silver Springs

ESTABLISHED: 2011

THE WHISKEYS: Small Batch Colorado Rye Whiskey; Small Batch Colorado Bourbon Whiskey; Barrel Proof Single Barrel Colorado Whiskey; Barrel Proof Single Barrel Bourbon Whiskey; Small Batch American Whiskey; Fresh Colorado Whiskey; White Dog Colorado Rye Whiskey; Bad Guy Colorado Bourbon Whiskey; HR Colorado Bourbon Whiskey; "E" Colorado Whiskey Experimental Series

THE STORY: Distillery 291 owner and founding distiller Michael Myers was a fashion and beauty photographer in New York until the events of September 11, 2001, convinced him to seek out a simpler life. Myers moved with his family to Colorado Springs, Colorado, where he built his first pot still using the copper photogravure plates he once used to make prints. It was exactly ten years later when the first drops of 291 Colorado dripped off the still. Myers's flagship 291 Colorado Whiskey Barrel Proof is a mash of malted rye and corn that's aged in white oak, finished with local Aspen wood staves, and bottled at barrel proof. 291's Experimental Whiskey series is a testing ground for special releases and potential line extensions. Their last E-Series release was single malt cut with beechwood-smoked malt and aged in ex-bourbon and ex-rye barrels.

The Family Jones, Loveland and Denver

ESTABLISHED: 2016

THE WHISKEYS: Ella Jones Bourbon; Atticus Jones Rye; Automatic Jones Rock & Rye; Jones House American Whiskey

THE STORY: Rob Masters has been craft distilling since 2007 and helped launch several start-ups, including Bently Heritage and Spring 44, before founding The Family Jones. The company's portfolio spans a gamut of spirits, including vodka, gin, rum, and a variety of bitters and liqueurs. But TFJ is best known for bourbon, rye, and rock-and-rye—a spiced, rye-based liqueur. TFJ has two locations. One is in Loveland, where Masters and his team process grains and distill, age, and blend their core spirits. The other is Spirit House in Denver, a slick cocktail bar, restaurant, and distillery. Here, Masters specializes in one-off experimental barrels, like corn whiskey distilled over a rack of pork ribs. Masters's latest release is Jones House American Whiskey, a blend of an eight-year-old stock distilled from a bourbon mash and a four-year straight rye.

Laws Whiskey House, Denver

ESTABLISHED: 2011

THE WHISKEYS: Four Grain Straight Bourbon; Four Grain Straight Bonded Bourbon; Four Grain Straight Cask Strength (Single Barrel) Bourbon; San Luis Valley Straight Rye; San Luis Valley Straight Bonded Rye; San Luis Valley Straight Cask Rye

THE STORY: Al Laws was a US Oil Services analyst before launching Laws Whiskey House in Denver. Laws sources grains from local farming families to make terroir-centric bourbon and rye. To jump-start the whiskey program, Laws hired former Barton 1792 master distiller Bill Friel, who taught Laws how to distill. The portfolio is a lineup of bourbons and ryes bottled straight cask strength (bonded), which are aged six years and bottled at 100 proof. Laws's signature bourbon is a wheat forward, four-grain recipe with a backdrop of rye and malted barley. Laws San Luis Valley Straight Rye is a spicy, in-your-face pure rye recipe bottled around four years. One swig of this stuff and you will KNOW you are drinking rye.

Old Elk, Fort Collins

ESTABLISHED: 2016

THE WHISKEY: Old Elk Bourbon Whiskey

THE STORY: Old Elk's Greg Metze began his career in 1978 at the old Seagram's plant in Lawrenceburg, Indiana. Today the plant is home to Midwest Grain Products (MGP), where Metze served as master distiller from 2007 to 2016. Metze was at MGP when he was hired by Old Elk founder and serial entrepreneur Curt Richardson to develop a signature bourbon. His only instruction: "Make it smooth and easy." To get there, Metze laid down a base of 51 percent corn, the minimum amount allowed in bourbon, then added 34 percent malt barley. (Most bourbons contain 5 percent or 10 percent malted barley.) Metze finished with a generous pinch of rye to punch up the spice and balance the flavors. In March 2020, the company added three new expressions to its portfolio: a five-year-old 95 percent rye, a straight wheated bourbon, and a 95 percent wheat whiskey. While Old Elk builds its distillery, its stocks are primarily contract distilled at MGP.

CHAPTER 5

FEW SPIRITS

HOW
PAUL HLETKO
EMERGED AS
THE KING
OF CRAFT WHISKEY
INNOVATION

THE DISTILLERY: FEW Spirits
ESTABLISHED: 2011
LOCATION: Evanston, Illinois
THE WHISKEYS: Straight Bourbon Whiskey; Straight Rye Whiskey; American Straight Whiskey; Cold Cut Bourbon; Single Malt Whiskey
WHY FEW MATTERS: Paul Hletko drove his own personal dagger into the belly of the temperance beast by launching his distillery in Evanston, Illinois, the birthplace of Prohibition. From its humble beginnings in 2011, Hletko grew his whiskey company from one lonely hybrid pot still in a back alley ex-chop shop into a world-class craft distillery that serves as a beacon of success for aspiring distillers. As his company expanded, so did his impact on the distilling community. Hletko is a former president of the American Craft Spirits Association and an advisory board member of DISCUS, and his brand has the distinction of being the first to be acquired by Samson & Surrey, a whole new kind of liquor company. His whiskey's pretty good too.

➺DRINKING, INTERRUPTED

It was right before the 2020 pandemic forced every bar and restaurant to shutter their doors that FEW founder Paul Hletko and I made plans to meet for drinks at Delilah's, a legendary bar in Chicago's Lincoln Park. This classic jukebox joint's owner, Mike Miller, has been building the bar's 800-plus whiskey list since Delilah's opened in 1993. It was around that time that Hletko started drinking here.

Had we been able to meet that day, we would have sipped FEW Spirits' Delilah's 23rd Anniversary batch. Hletko, Miller, and others from the Delilah's team spent three days tasting and playing with endless combinations of FEW bourbon, rye, and other stocks to strike upon the expression. Only 23 barrels, or 1,812 bottles, were released. This wasn't the first collaborative bottling Hletko has engineered, and it won't be the last.

As a kid, Hletko used to walk with his grandfather along the lakeside of Michigan Avenue, past the Drake Hotel, a place Hletko calls "the most

MEET THE MAKER:
FEW FOUNDER
PAUL HLETKO

Chicago thing in Chicago to have ever Chicago-ed." He would stare in awe at the fancy people doing fancy things inside the Drake, dreaming to be fancy there himself one day. Hletko couldn't have known his whiskey journey would eventually lead him back to the Drake one day, but that's exactly what happened.

➨CZECHOSLOVAKIA, 1939

FEW Spirits opened its doors in 2011, but the distillery's history begins long before Hletko was even born. The story starts in 1939, when Germany occupied Czechoslovakia at the onset of World War II. Hletko's family owned a successful brewery in what is now the Czech Republic when the Nazis invaded, confiscating the business and herding the family into concentration camps. Alfred Dube, Hletko's grandfather, was the only survivor. When the war ended, Dube came to the United States via Ellis Island. He never had the chance to reclaim his family's birthright, his beloved brewery.

Paul Hletko wore many hats before he made his way to whiskey: professional guitar player, record label owner, and patent lawyer, a paper-pushing desk job he hated. But what drove Hletko to discover his true calling was the passing of his grandfather in 2008. Determined to honor his family's brewing legacy, Hletko combined his love for art, business, and family to create an empire that would make Alfred Dube proud.

➨PEORIA WAS A WHISKEY TOWN UNTIL IT WASN'T

There were already a dozen or so breweries around Chicago when Hletko began researching a business investment in 2008. The craft beer scene was saturated, but there were only two distilleries in the area and only a few dozen scattered around the United States. It was still early in the craft spirits awakening. The movement was quietly gaining traction as American whiskey, primarily bourbon, was getting hot in the marketplace. The idea of creating a whiskey company in the heart of America's breadbasket gave Hletko chills. Here was his chance to resurrect the rich, pre-Prohibition whiskey heritage in Illinois, a state that had a booming distilling industry in the 19th century.

Smack in the center of the United States sits Peoria, Illinois, once the largest distilling city in the country. Quality water, abundant grains, an emerging railroad system, and access to the Illinois River—a tributary of

What's in the Bottle? FEW Bourbon

THE VITALS: Non-age-stated; 46.5% ABV/93 proof; mash bill: 70% corn, 20% rye, 10% malted barley. Non-chill-filtered.

PROCESS: FEW whiskeys are created in the purest spirit of the craft credo, meaning Hletko unapologetically makes whiskey that makes sense to him, not what Kentucky traditions dictate. Hletko was a home brewer for twenty years, and he brings a brewer's mentality to distilling. Unlike the distiller's yeast commonly used in industrial whiskey production, Hletko ferments with a Belgian beer yeast, then uses a column still for the first distillation before finishing the whiskey in a copper hybrid pot. The distillate comes off at 137 proof and enters the bottle at 93.5 in honor of the 1893 World's Fair in Chicago, where Francis Elizabeth Willard, an anti-alcohol activist, was a featured speaker. FEW used to be aged in 15- and 30-gallon oak barrels but has since switched over to standard 53-gallon barrels, which are sourced from Barrel Mill in Minnesota.

TASTE: FEW Bourbon has a high-but-not-too-high rye content, which lends a spicy kick to the corn's sweetness, backed up with hints of vanilla from the barrel and spices like cinnamon, black pepper, and clove. These are present from the nose through the finish.

the Mississippi—all contributed to the emergence of Peoria's alcohol industry. Peoria alone produced 18 million gallons of alcohol in 1880, three million more than all of Kentucky. Good times rolled in Illinois from the mid-century until the once-mighty Peoria liquor hub was hobbled by the dismantling of the Whiskey Trust and then knocked out by Prohibition.

THE WHISKEY TRUST

The 1880s were unpredictable times for the liquor industry. The ever-escalating excise tax, originally established to help fund the War of 1812 and later the Civil War, contributed to erratic market swings volatile enough to wipe out start-up liquor producers who gambled on favorable short-term economic conditions (a lesson best heeded by modern craft distillers). The solution was the Distillers' and Cattle Feeders' Trust, or the Whiskey Trust, founded in Peoria, Illinois. The Whiskey Trust was a committee of trustees—mostly shady whiskey rectifiers, really—whose business model was purchasing competing companies, shuttering most of them, and operating what was left as one massive corporation.

By 1890 the trust was in possession of about 80 percent of the United States whiskey market. This gave it a lot of power, power it exercised by price fixing and bullying brands within the trust who didn't meet sales quotas, sometimes with dynamite. The trust eventually began buckling under its own weight before it was disbanded with the passing of the Sherman Anti-Trust Act in 1895. The trust revived on a smaller scale in 1899, but it never returned to its former dominance and fizzled out in time.

➥ DESECRATING THE BIRTHPLACE OF PROHIBITION

After scraping together enough capital to launch his business on a shoestring, Hletko's next step was finding the perfect location. He chose Evanston, Illinois, his own neighborhood and possibly the last place on earth anyone would dare build a distillery. Located on Chicago's northern border, Evanston isn't just a historically dry town. It's also home to the Women's Christian Temperance Union, making this essentially the birthplace of Prohibition. (Technically, the union was founded in Ohio, but it came to prominence when it moved to Evanston.)

Evanston resident Francis Elizabeth Willard was a vocal union leader in the anti-alcohol movement in the years leading up to the 18th Amendment, which established the prohibition of alcohol in the United States. It's commonly accepted that FEW was named in mock honor of Willard, whose initials spell out FEW. Hletko denies it, claiming he never thought he would make a lot of whiskeys—the plan was to only make a few. But if a journalist prints it as truth, which happens often, Hletko spends no time correcting them. There's whiskey to make.

Hletko may have planned to only make a few barrels, but he would soon be making a shitload. While his first bourbon and rye stocks aged, he released his first product: gin. This allowed him to enter the market in 2011, relatively soon after launch, and the timing could not have been better. The cocktail scene was in full swing already, and American whiskey as a category was exploding. DISCUS data shows that sales of super-premium bourbon had jumped a million cases to 8.7 million in the two years since FEW launched. Clearly, we Americans were looking for new and exciting things to drink. Craft was still in its infancy, but gone were the days that nobody knew what it was. This was largely thanks to a vodka guy named Tito Beveridge in Austin, Texas, who grew his home-spun Tito's Vodka brand from a pipe dream to a 10-million-case juggernaut. Distributors in search of the next silver bullet began courting Hletko. Things were happening.

➤➤THE GOLDEN DAYS OF CRAFT

Hletko hit his five-year sales goal in less than two years and his ten-year projection in five. This growth level required the business to grow more quickly than expected, which is no doubt an excellent problem to have, but it's still a problem. He expanded his team, adding more distillers and market ambassadors and filling out the bottling and barreling crew. The equipment had to be upgraded, as well—Hletko was forced to swap out his tiny pot stills for one four times the size, and from there came additional fermenters, an upgraded mash tank, and finally a pricey stainless column still. Despite the upgrades, it would be years before the distillery would catch up to demand.

To give you an idea of that demand, FEW was filling only 5 or 10 percent of its orders in 2014. When Hletko landed a quarter-million-dollar purchase order by a distributor, he could only fill $3,000 in product. He just didn't have the inventory to make it happen—one reason so many small producers struggle to grow. This leads one to beg the question: How do you finance a business where you have to pay upfront and then wait several years before your product can enter the marketplace? Unless you have unlimited funds, which Hletko certainly did not, your options are to give up equity or take on debt. Hletko had already sacrificed both. Something needed to change.

During this time, a mutual friend brokered a meeting between Hletko and Robert Furniss-Roe, a founder of Samson & Surrey. Furniss-Roe and his partner, Juan Rovira, are ex-Bacardi execs who had been working on a fresh concept of liquor brand ownership that operates more like a commune than a corporation. In a typical big-box conglomerate acquisition, brand owners are commonly paid a fee for the sale of the brand or distillery. The previous owners are put on contract as "consultants" and remain the face of the brand for the duration of the deal, usually five years. The Samson & Surrey model, however, stipulates that producers agree to sell their brand to the company in exchange for a partnership in the company's entire portfolio of spirits in perpetuity.

⇒→SAMSON & SURREY TAKES ROOT

In 2016 FEW became the first company to join forces with Samson & Surrey. With the stroke of a pen, Hletko suddenly had access to sufficient operating capital, a professional marketing team, and all the other stuff he previously had to figure out on his own. Most importantly, Samson & Surrey had a global sales force that is today a 45-member team. Hletko no longer worries about the logistics of filling orders in France. Now it's the European sales manager's job to make that happen. Hletko is free to focus on his whiskey and represent all the brands that eventually joined the Samson & Surrey portfolio. At the time of writing, the collection includes Brenne French Whiskey, Tequila Ocho, Bluecoat Gin, Widow Jane Bourbon, Mezcal Vago, and FEW. The arrangement has a casual, friendly vibe—these partners pool their resources to support one another on every level, representing each other in tastings, trade shows, and sales calls. Jumping into this agreement was a bold move for Hletko, but it was a risk he was willing to take to bring his product to the next level. And what exactly does the next level mean?

Since the day Hletko decided to sell a "few" bottles of whiskey in his grandfather's honor, the brand has grown to become the second highest selling craft bourbon in the United States (behind Hudson Baby, powered by William Grant & Sons). As of the spring of 2020, FEW hovers at the top of every craft category out there. For Hletko, the next level means removing the "craft" modifier in order to compete with large-scale producers in the general market. According to Hletko, he already does, citing large brands that have begun taking cues from FEW and other innovative craft producers. (You can say it's a coincidence that a certain Tennessee rye came out four years after Hletko's with an identical mash bill to FEW's 70 rye, 20 corn, 10 malt barley recipe, but Hletko isn't so sure.)

FEW'S TASTING ROOM WOULD BE FROWNED UPON BY THE TOWN'S TEMPERANCE-MINDED FOUNDERS.

THIS BOURBON, BARRELED IN APRIL 2017, WILL LIKELY BE HITTING THE BOTTLE SOON.

As for Hletko's childhood dream of someday being fancy at the Drake Hotel, consider it realized. More than three decades after he walked past the hotel with his grandfather, Hletko became ambassador of the Coq d'Or, a private drinking club at the Drake, where he's created multiple rye expressions exclusive to the club. Over time, Hletko has become known for his partnerships and experimentation: His passion for coffee inspired him to create Cold Cut Brew, in which the bourbon is brought to proof with coffee instead of water, and his deep love for music led him to work on special bottlings with bands like the Flaming Lips and Alice in Chains. While the industry pins a marketing badge on Hletko for FEW's sometimes out-there collaborations, winning marketer awards and grabbing media attention was never the point. At the end of the day, Hletko simply wants to be known to all as a guy who makes great whiskey.

FIVE BEST IN
THE MIDWEST

It certainly makes sense to distill whiskey in the Midwest, considering the entire grain supply chain is centered around the region. In the past decade, about 20 craft distilleries and production companies have popped up throughout the Midwest. Here are a few of the best.

Templeton, Templeton, Iowa

ESTABLISHED: 2006

THE WHISKEYS: 4-Year Rye; 6-Year Rye; Barrel Strength; Special Reserve 10-Year; Maple Cask Finish

THE STORY: You can't tell the story of craft distilling without mentioning Templeton. These guys deserve credit for being the first on the craft scene to boldly launch a super-premium rye, and the move paid off. Whiskey geeks loved this new Iowa-style rye, a spirit few had ever considered ordering before Templeton rocked the whiskey world with this killer stuff. Then Templeton's reputation took a hit when it was revealed that the Iowa rye wasn't made in Iowa at all. It was a purchased whiskey made by Midwest Grain Products (MGP) in Indiana. The ensuing blowback was bad for Templeton, who since have come clean about the origins of their product and constructed an Iowa distillery in 2017. While that juice ages, Templeton has a beautiful collection of age-stated ryes that may be sourced but taste damn good.

StilL 630, St. Louis, Missouri

ESTABLISHED: 2011

THE WHISKEYS: RallyPoint Rye; Big Jake White Dog; Big Jake Breakfast Brew; 5-Year RallyPoint Single Barrel Rye; S.S. Sorghum Whiskey; Monon Bell Bourbon; The Truth American Single Malt; RallyPoint Rye Wine Cask

THE STORY: StilL 630 is a St. Louis–centric distillery inside what used to be a Hardee's restaurant, located three blocks south of Busch Stadium. Proprietor David Weglarz dedicated his distillery to his beloved city by naming it 630 in homage to the 630-foot St. Louis Arch. It's also the day Weglarz launched the company—June 30, 2011—and the serial number of their Missouri-made pot still. 630's program runs a gamut of styles from bourbon and rye to single malt and includes the first Bottled-in-Bond whiskey to come out of Missouri. But the hidden gem is a 100 percent sorghum whiskey. Sorghum is a tall cane grass plant similar to sugar cane that's occasionally used to make specialty rums (most rum is made from molasses) and Chinese baijiu. Weglarz also collaborates with local brewers to distill their beer into unique whiskeys. This attention to community and passion for fine product draws much love from the craft industry and earned StilL 360 the Whiskey of the Year designation from the ACSA in 2016 and 2018.

Koval, Chicago, Illinois

ESTABLISHED: 2008

THE WHISKEYS: Single Barrel Bourbon; White Whiskey Rye; Single Barrel Rye; Single Barrel Millet; Single Barrel Oat; Single Barrel Four Grain

THE STORY: Before building Koval in Chicago in 2008, Dr. Robert Birnecker served as the deputy press secretary for the Austrian Embassy in Washington, DC, but distillation has always been in his blood. After growing up at his grandparents' winery and distillery in Austria, Birnecker became a distillation educator and consultant who has helped launch almost 200 craft distilleries. When Birnecker opened Koval, he was considered eccentric for his commitment to organic ingredients and funky alternate grains. His signature bourbon is made with 51 percent corn (the lowest possible corn content to be called a bourbon) and 49 percent millet. Koval Four Grain is distilled from a mash of corn, rye, millet, and oat. All Koval whiskeys are bottled as single barrels and are aged in 30-gallon casks between two and four years.

Cedar Ridge, Swisher, Iowa

ESTABLISHED: 2005

THE WHISKEYS: Iowa Straight Bourbon; Single Malt Whiskey; Malted Rye; Wheat Whiskey; Reserve Iowa Bourbon; Slipknot No. 9 Bourbon; Slipknot No. 9 Iowa Whiskey

THE STORY: Iowa produces more corn than anywhere else in the country, but when Cedar Ridge CEO and distiller Jeff Quint decided to obtain the first distillery license in Iowa since Prohibition, Hawkeyes were sourcing 100 percent of their whiskey from out of state. Cedar Ridge features a little bit of everything in its whiskey stable, including bourbon, wheat whiskey, single malt, and rye. But the coolest whiskey in the stable is No. 9, created in collaboration with M. Shawn "Clown" Crahan from the metal band Slipknot. Quint and Crahan worked together to blend bourbon and rye stocks into what whiskey critic Fred Minnick called "the most interesting whiskey ever to come out of Iowa."

J. Henry & Sons, Dane, Wisconsin

ESTABLISHED: 2009

THE WHISKEYS: Small Batch 92 Proof Bourbon; Patton Road Reserve Cask Strength; Bellefontaine Reserve Cognac Finished

THE STORY: Joe Henry and his sons grow and mill the heirloom rye, wheat, and red corn found in J. Henry's signature four-grain bourbon on their 900-acre family farm, located 20 miles north of Madison, Wisconsin. To create this unique bourbon, Henry revitalized a corn strain that grew in the fields during his childhood by tapping the University of Wisconsin to give him 1,200 seeds that had sat dormant since the mid-70s. These homegrown grains are contract distilled off-site. The distillate is then returned to the farm, where it's matured five years inside a converted 100-year-old dairy barn, subject to Wisconsin's dramatic weather swings. J. Henry laid down their first batch of rye in 2019, which is slated to join their bourbon lineup in a couple of years. Meanwhile, sons Joe and Jack are planning a distillery to bring their operation entirely in-house.

A Few Reasons Craft Whiskey Seems Expensive

DRINKERS ARE KNOWN TO EXPERIENCE STICKER SHOCK over the price of craft whiskey, and truth be told, I used to feel that way too. What makes it so expensive?

1. Economy of scale: The cost of grains is based on quantity—the more you purchase the less you pay. This law of scale applies to every aspect of production, including barrels, labels, bottles, and corks.

2. Location, location, location: Certain states, like Kentucky and Tennessee, are perfectly situated for easy access to corn. But a distiller in Alaska, for example, will pay over ten-fold the freight cost for the same parcel. This turns into big money.

3. Seed-to-glass is an expensive, risky business model: Grain-to-glass distilleries are often, but not always, run by professional farmers. But when growing your own grains, it's important to grow to the level of quality that competitors are purchasing from grain brokers. If your crop falls short, your production cost skyrockets. This is especially true for upstart fields where farmers are still working out kinks and seasoning their soil. Storing grain is another consideration. If it gets musty, you have issues. On the other hand, if you don't like what the broker sends you, back it goes.

4. Even non-distillery products feel the pinch: Purchasing finished whiskey for bottling or contract distilling will have a higher cost by nature. Large contract distillers like Midwest Grain Products (MGP) in Indiana have the ability to make whiskey more efficiently than craft distillers, but they don't give the stuff away. The upcharge will always affect the bottom line, and a blender or bottler of sourced products needs to charge more for a tighter margin than the actual producers they compete against. The advantages? A shorter cash flow cycle, a far less chance you will run out of stock, and you don't need to age the stuff. If you need whiskey right away, you can order it.

5. The mom-and-pop shop dilemma: There are plenty of small family distilleries throughout the United States that make a fine living from tourist traffic, but then again, there are many who struggle to attract attention. More tourist-heavy towns command higher rent and foster competition, while those in more rural areas find they need to spend more to promote their business and invest in additional revenue drivers like event spaces. As the market saturates, these escalating promotion costs cut deep.

CHAPTER 6

BALCONES

HOW A LONE STAR STATE DISTILLERY HELPED PUT TEXAS WHISKY ON THE MAP

THE DISTILLERY: Balcones

ESTABLISHED: 2008

LOCATION: Waco, Texas

THE WHISKEYS: Baby Blue Corn Whisky; Texas Single Malt; Texas Pot Still Bourbon; True Blue; Brimstone; Texas Rye; Texas Bourbon; Lineage Single Malt

WHY BALCONES MATTERS: Balcones was one of the early craft movement's most accomplished distilleries, created with the goal of producing whisky with the elegant character of single malt and the personality of a Texas cowboy. Balcones was meteoric in its rise, spectacular in its crash, and phoenix-like in its resurrection. Sounds dramatic, and it is. But the story of Balcones is also one of passion for whisky and a do-it-yourself approach to realizing your dreams.

⇥MEET THE PLAYERS

Charles "Chip" Tate was born in Lynchburg, Virginia, where he began home brewing as a teenager, fermenting "beer" out of wheat germ, flour, and other grains found in his kitchen. After studying at the College of William and Mary and the Union Theological Seminary, Tate relocated to Waco, Texas. There, he worked at Baylor University and launched a tech company before making his way to the Institute of Brewing and Distilling. In 2006, Tate earned a master-level diploma in both, setting him on the path to becoming a distiller. It wasn't long before Tate was at a junk shop, hunting for pieces to create his first still.

Jared Himstedt has a face for Texas whisky—edgy long hair, an unruly beard, and thick gauges in his ears. As a kid, Himstedt split time between Texas and Brazil, where his father worked in a seminary as a music missionary. Eventually Himstedt settled in Texas permanently and studied social work and ceramics at Baylor. Outside of school, he played guitar in punk and rock bands around Waco. He also became an aficionado of single malt scotch right around the time that the local craft beer scene was exploding. Himstedt caught the brewing bug and started making beer at home. In 2006, he became manager of the Dancing Bear, a friend's craft

TEXAS PROUD:
BALCONES DISTILLER
JARED HIMSTEDT

beer bar. The plan was to convert the beer bar to a brewpub, where Himstedt would make the beer. The beer bar was a success, but for whatever reason, the brewery never happened. Himstedt began poking around for another opportunity. Something creative.

⇒⇒LIFTOFF

Tate and Himstedt met through a brewers club in Waco in 2005 and bonded over a mutual interest in beermaking and a love for single malt scotch. Tate became a regular at the Dancing Bear, hanging out with Himstedt while planning what would become Balcones, a whisky company the likes of which Texas had never known.

Tate's first pot still was a tall, funky-shaped, stove-top affair cobbled together with odd parts and copper sheet metal. Initial experiments were a mash of peated and unpeated malt, made in Tate's kitchen. Tate and Himstedt occasionally sipped this Texas shine with friends on Himstedt's back porch.

On one such night in 2008, Tate was introduced to Steve Germer, the brother-in-law of a mutual friend and a potential investor. Tate laid out his vision for creating a Texas single malt distillery, and Germer was impressed. After a few subsequent meetings, Germer invested about $100,000 and became a partner. Tate maxed out his credit cards, took out a personal loan, and borrowed from friends (including Himstedt) to purchase a 3,000-square-foot ex-welding shop underneath a bridge on 17th Street in Waco and construct a distillery. Balcones was in business.

⇒⇒GET IN THE MUCK AND FIGURE IT OUT

Every single thing in the ex-welding shop on 17th Street needed to be retrofitted, modified, or fixed. There was zero budget for plumbers, electricians, or technicians, so before his evening shifts at the Dancing Bear, Himstedt worked at the distillery all day, learning how to install insulation,

WHISKEY VS. WHISKY:
The Not-So-Curious Case of the Missing "e"

As a rule of thumb, the Scottish spell *whisky* without an "e," while Ireland and the United States include it. However, there is no rule to this, and several domestic brands drop the "e," McCarthy's, Maker's Mark, and Balcones among them. For this reason, *whisky* is spelled in the Scotch style in this chapter.

THE BALCONES DISTILLERY WAS ORIGINALLY THE TEXAS FIREPROOF STORAGE BUILDING, BUILT IN THE 1920S.

piping systems, and burners. After months of burning the candle at both ends, Himstedt joined Balcones full-time.

Then there was equipment to buy. Tate purchased a pair of alembic-style Portuguese brandy stills, which he eventually rebuilt piece by piece. Other "equipment" came mostly from eBay and Craigslist, like inexpensive containers that they welded lids on top of to use as fermenters. This do-it-yourself approach was adopted as a way of life at Balcones: Don't buy what you can make yourself.

Working at Balcones was like working in an artist's studio—Tate was the artist and the whisky was the art. The style of art could be called "anti-traditionalist." This doesn't mean Tate didn't respect tradition. Everything Balcones does stands on the shoulders of what others have done before. But it does mean that Tate approached whisky based on what he believed was the right whisky to make, without influences from conventional producers in Scotland or Kentucky. He knew that if he was going to stand out, he needed to be himself.

Himstedt, meanwhile, took on the role of production manager at the distillery, providing structure by scheduling staff, paying invoices, and assuring the trains ran on time. With few staff in the early days, everyone did a little bit of everything, including spending hours at the stills, smelling and tasting and adjusting the run as the day went on. Himstedt also designed Balcones's original logo.

Little did anybody realize that this little Texas craft distillery would soon explode. When the original investor, Steve Germer, became de facto head of sales, he began peddling this local whisky throughout Texas while also working to bring Balcones to other markets like Seattle, San Francisco, and New York.

➤➤AND THE SKY TURNED BABY BLUE

Balcones released Texas Baby Blue in March 2009. Baby Blue is classified as a corn whisky, not a bourbon, and was bottled after only a few months of aging. Blue corn is a specialized variety with a Native American and southwestern tradition that stretches back thousands of years. For Balcones, it made sense to work with a grain that could deliver a distinctive Southwest flavor—it added a Texas twist to the whisky.

The local crowd was receptive to Baby Blue, but for an expert opinion, Balcones entered the 2009 San Francisco World Spirits Competition, a prestigious program where spirits are evaluated by a panel of expert tasters. Balcones stunned critics and the craft community when Baby Blue scored double gold, the highest medal. The experts who once scoffed at the notion of Texas whisky suddenly had their cups out. A parade of magazines and newspapers heaped accolades on Balcones, in one case proclaiming Baby Blue the "Best Corn Whiskey on the Planet." Balcones had arrived, and they were just warming up.

The year 2009 was a fertile one for the young distillery. Despite the learning curve that all start-up distilleries face, they quickly developed an impressive portfolio of spirits. Rumble, a concoction of distilled honey, sugar, and fig, was released around the same time as Baby Blue. Next up was Brimstone, a Texan riff on peaty single malt scotch smoked with scrub oak, a local wood used in Texas barbeque. The following year, Balcones released their signature American Single Malt and True Blue, a more mature Baby Blue. With two small stills and five products to make, the Balcones team was working those old brandy stills to death. And when the equipment ran perfectly, which was never a guarantee, Balcones could just make enough money to not go bankrupt.

➤→REELING IN THE BIG FISH

By 2010, it became clear that for Balcones to grow as a company, they would need to make more whisky, which meant they needed more hardware and a larger space. To that end, Germer brought in Michael Rockafellow, a friend and investor who became a partner, kicking in a seven-figure investment between 2010 and 2012. With this investment, Balcones purchased a four-story, 60,000-square-foot brick warehouse on 11th Street. The massive space was initially used to store aging barrels, but the end goal was to build a distillery inside the space. To do so would require a multimillion-dollar investment, exponentially more money than anything Balcones had raised in the past. But by now, Balcones was a known entity with upward trending sales in an exploding whisky market. Surely they would attract bigger fish.

As for the hardware, there are many craftsmen out there who make pot stills. They're a relatively simple contraption. But there are just a handful of stillhouses that build large-format stills designed to make massive quantities of high-quality spirits. Forsyths in Scotland arguably makes the finest in the world, but as much as Tate dreamed of ordering a pair of Forsyths copper pots, the $300,000 price tag was out of his range. Instead, Tate purchased $80,000 worth of copper and designed his own stills, using tools that were borderline medieval. Spent oxygen tanks were used to roll copper into a tube as they set a sheet metal pattern and stretched metal. Tate's first two stills were shaped identically to the direct-fire alembic Portuguese stills but built with thicker gauge copper for more durability.

Tate built these stills out of necessity, but once he started understanding how a vessel's design influences a whisky's characteristics, he was hooked almost in a spiritual way. In his view, making whisky in a still you built yourself is the craft's apex, where distilling and still-making are part and parcel. The way he describes it, "You understand connections between the vessel and the distillate that allows you a broader palette of possibilities in which to create."

When the new stills came online in March 2014, Balcones jumped from producing 125 gallons of distillate per week to 100 gallons every day.

➤→LEVEL UP

Things were going well on the distilling front but winds of change began blowing on the business side as Balcones took on a new investor.

Greg Allen is a Harvard-trained attorney and the former CEO of a privately held food processing company that he and his partners grew to over $750 million in revenue, then sold in 2010. Allen was introduced to Tate when Allen was flirting with investing in Virginia Distilling Company. Mutual friends recommended that Allen check out Balcones before moving forward. Allen visited Waco in February 2013 and spent the day eating lunch, sipping whisky, and talking shop with the Balcones crew. Afterward, Tate pitched Allen the idea of joining Balcones. Negotiations ensued, and a deal was struck. Allen became a majority investor, Tate remained president and head distiller, and the multimillion-dollar distillery project on 11th Street was a go.

➤➤A FORK IN THE ROAD

During the preconstruction phase for the new distillery, it became clear that the project would far exceed projections and run well past the agreed-upon timeline. The reality of these ballooning costs sparked a rift between Allen and Tate that resulted in a nasty court battle where irreconcilable differences led to divorce. Tate and Allen settled in December 2014, resulting in Tate selling his shares and exiting Balcones.

Amid this drama, the 11th Street location was under construction. Himstedt assumed the role of distillery manager during the transition, doing his best to manage production in the original facility while reworking the plans for the new distillery. Allen's investment finally afforded the company equipment that they could grow into. In the new space, a team from Forsyths installed an 8,000-liter copper pot and a mash cooker once belonging to Speyburn, a single malt distillery near Rothes, Scotland. In early 2015, Balcones moved into their gorgeous, cutting-edge distillery, complete with tasting room and gift shop. Himstedt and the crew laid down as much juice as possible, and capacity increased by almost tenfold. In 2016, Himstedt officially changed his title to head distiller.

What's the Difference Between Corn Whisky and Bourbon?

The TTB defines corn whisky as being made from at least 80 percent corn, aged in used or uncharred barrels. Bourbon must contain a minimum of 51 percent corn and is matured in new charred oak containers. Corn whisky also tends to be drunk at a younger age than most bourbon and therefore tends to be sweeter with dominant creamed corn and raw cereal characteristics.

The Craft of the Pot Still by Chip Tate

"Most people don't think much about how their whisky is made, which is all very well, until you're a pot-still maker trying to explain what the hell it is you do—and that's me.

"So what does a pot-still maker do? We use torches large enough to rattle the neighbors' windows to heat thick sheets of copper until they glow hot, then beat them with heavy rawhide hammers into beautiful multi-ton copper cauldrons with sexy curves. These pots are joined together with electric welding machines with such precision that the edges match up within a coin's thickness for the final joining across diameters as large as 12 feet. Finally, the pot is planished to yield the final shape and the faceted surface of the pot.

"The point of it all? To produce distillate with the guts to lay down in barrels and create a fine whisky. The crafts of distilling and making pot stills are both a dance in chapters, carefully worked in minutes and over years with slow, steady-handed confidence toward a goal beyond sight but worth reaching. That is what we do."

Aging Whisky in Texas:
A Ridiculously Simplified Explanation
by Jared Himstedt

"The barrel and the climate have everything to do with how a whisky matures. Scotch is generally aged in used barrels in a colder, more temperate environment. Bourbon, conversely, matures in new oak barrels in a climate filled with hot days and cold nights, where heat forces liquid inside the wood, through the layers of char and toast, then expels the distillate as the wood's pores tighten up in the cold.

"There was no whisky history in Texas when Balcones launched, so nobody knew how whisky would mature in the hot, damp Waco environment. We learned quickly that the persistent heat facilitates deeper wood penetration and the wild temperature swings move the whisky in and out of the wood more quickly than other environments. This is great for infusing flavor into the liquid quickly, but it tends to introduce over-oaked flavor and heavy tannin.

"Through years of experimentation we learned that achieving a balanced whisky in this hot climate requires a longer fermentation time with lower final pH than classic scotch or bourbon. It's a little less efficient, but this provides a host of fruity, floral aromas and flavors to complement the wood notes. We also use larger barrels and a variety of entry proofs to maintain the delicate balance of extraction and development."

⇥MOVING FORWARD

Back in the day, Tate and Himstedt planned on experimenting with a laundry list of whisky styles, but it was tough to justify making new stuff when they couldn't keep up with demand for the whisky they already had. But now Himstedt had the space to be creative. His first innovations included wheated and high-rye bourbons, rye, and peated malt, which became the next additions to the growing Balcones portfolio. Over the next four years, Himstedt immersed himself in research and development by experimenting with dozens of additional innovations. These projects resulted in adding a rye, a pot-still bourbon, and Lineage, Balcones's newest single malt, to the core lineup, plus another five annual single malt releases.

It's the experimental program for which Balcones, and Himstedt, have become best known. In 2020 alone, Balcones released more than twenty different products, including funky grain recipes and exotic barrel finishes, on top of full line-product extensions. At the time of writing, the shiny new

What's in the Bottle?
Balcones Single Malt

THE VITALS: 100% malted barley; triple wood aged; non-age-stated (NAS). ABV: 53% (106 proof); non-chill-filtered.

PROCESS: Balcones's flagship single malt fuses traditional old-world single malt with American-style maturation. Golden Promise malted barley is combined with a classic scotch yeast for a 7-to-10-day open fermentation. This wash undergoes double distillation in a traditional Scottish pot still. Distillate comes off the still at about 70% alcohol. Balcones then takes a page from the American bourbon playbook by maturing the majority of what enters the bottle in oversized 59-gallon, virgin charred-oak barrels. The balance of the blend is aged in ex-bourbon barrels with a touch of French oak.

TASTE: A fruit-laden nose is loaded with stone fruit, banana, and pear with hints of honey, rose, and citrus. The taste is like fresh buttered bread and jammy fruit, with a silky viscosity that fills the mouth and affords a long, smooth finish.

whisky toy at Balcones is Texas-grown barley. Don't be surprised if it starts popping up, at least as a limited edition.

Over time, Himstedt has become an industry leader. He was named the Master Distiller of the Year in 2019 by the Icons of Whisky America, was elected by his peers to be the first president of the Texas Whiskey Association, and serves as a founding member of the American Single Malt Whiskey Commission. Balcones is also now one of the fastest-growing whisky brands in the country.

➠PHOENIX RISES

In July 2020, Chip Tate put the finishing touches on one of the six pot stills he crafted inside his maker's space, which sits on a 27.5-acre property tucked between Lake Waco and the airport, just inside the city limits. This is the headquarters for Tate's two new companies. The first is Chip Tate Craft Copperworks, purveyors of large-scale copper pot stills. With each strike of the hammer, Tate moves closer toward his goal of becoming a master pot-still craftsmen, a distinction few have earned. The other side of the building is home to Tate & Co., a distillery Tate has been slowly and carefully building since late 2016. After learning from his experience with Balcones, Tate is taking care to build a distillery with the ability to scale up. He plans to soon be selling a whole lot of whisky.

THE ON-SITE TASTING ROOM IS MADE IN PART FROM MATERIALS RECLAIMED FROM THE ORIGINAL BUILDING.

BALCONES'S
FORSYTH WASH
STILLS ARE 12,500
AND 13,500
LITERS, STANDING
30 FEET TALL.

TEXAS FIREWATER

A Spotlight on Garrison Bros. (Hye, Texas)

LONG BEFORE THE BALCONES boys ever dreamed of making whiskey in the Lone Star State, Garrison Bros. proprietor Dan Garrison was already blazing a trail for a new Texan tradition.

Garrison began fantasizing about making Texas bourbon two decades ago after his software company collapsed in the Enron accounting scandal, an event resulting in thousands losing their jobs and life savings. The idea became serious when Garrison embarked on a fact-finding mission to the Kentucky Bourbon Trail. His assessment was that a handful of companies were making every brand on the back bar and there wasn't much in the way of variation. "There was Wild Turkey 80 proof and Wild Turkey 101 proof," he says. "Same stuff. Then you had Beam's small batch collection, Booker's, Baker's and Knob Creek, just variations on the same bourbon. I saw through these thinly veiled marketing efforts and saw an opportunity to create something truly original and authentic. Thus began my journey down bourbon road."

It was 2006 when Garrison purchased Buffalo Trace's 100-gallon experimental still from Vendome Brass and Copper in Louisville, a vessel he named the Copper Cowgirl. He built a 1,000-square-foot distillery on a 68-acre parcel of land in the Texas Hill Country that was purchased by his mother-in-law and received his distilling license in 2007, becoming the first legal whiskey distillery in Texas.

Garrison Bros. has grown steadily by starting locally and sprawling out from there. Garrison sold his first 2,000 bottles in nearby Blanco and Gillespie counties in 2010, then

THE HEART OF HILL COUNTRY: GARRISON BROS. DISTILLERY

DAN GARRISON

expanded to Austin, San Antonio, Houston, and Dallas/Fort Worth between 2011 and 2015. Garrison doubled down on his bourbon production in 2017, adding a 2,000-gallon pot still from Vendome Brass and Copper that he cheekily named the Big Johnson, allegedly after Lyndon B. Johnson, who grew up in nearby Johnson City. As of 2021, Garrison's Small Batch bourbons are available in 35 states and 6 foreign countries.

Along the way, Garrison has reluctantly adopted a superhero role in the craft community, fighting corruption wherever he sees it. In his opinion, corruption exists at every tier of liquor distribution because the laws in every American state differ and are in conflict; most were written into law between 1933 and 1935 by the same families that controlled liquor distribution during Prohibition. Garrison is a vocal member of the ACSA, ADI, the Texas Distilled Spirits Association, and the Texas Whiskey Association. "I have helped to create and fund industry associations that lobby on behalf of small craft spirits makers," he says. "In this industry, the tail is wagging the dog. That has put a target on my back but I have no regrets. I get to drink good bourbon with new friends every evening, so I have the greatest job in the world."

GARRISON BROS. WHISKEYS: Texas Straight Small Batch Bourbon; Single Barrel Bourbon; Cowboy Uncut and Unfiltered Bourbon; Balmorhea Twice-Barreled Bourbon; Laguna Madre Limousin Oak-Immersed Straight Bourbon; Honeydew Honey-Infused Straight Bourbon; Estacado Port-Finished Straight Bourbon

CHAPTER 7

CORSAIR

HOW ANDREW WEBBER AND DAREK BELL BROUGHT SMALL-BATCH DISTILLING BACK TO TENNESSEE

THE DISTILLERY: Corsair
ESTABLISHED: 2008
LOCATION: Nashville, Tennessee
THE WHISKEYS: Triple Smoke; Dark Rye
WHY CORSAIR MATTERS: In the distillery, malt house, smokehouse, and barrel house, Darek Bell and Andrew Webber have distilled, prototyped, and cataloged thousands of whiskey variations with an emphasis on malt, alternative grains, and smoke. After spending over a decade meticulously recording the findings of their experiments, Bell and Webber released their secrets to the world in an effort to inform and educate distillers who came after them. Corsair is a role model for taking risks and sharing valuable research to give back to the craft movement.

⇥BOUND BY SCIENCE

Andrew Webber and Darek Bell met the first day of high school in Nashville, Tennessee, but it would be a few years before they became friends. Eventually, they found themselves moving in similar circles and sharing interests in biology, ecology, and conservation. They began partnering on science projects, first for class and then outside of school, running experiments like building an enclosed ecosystem in Bell's front yard with plants and freshwater crustaceans in a giant glass ball. The ecosystem was supposed to sustain itself for 20 years, but his mom put her foot down and made them get rid of it.

After high school, Webber studied biology at Rice University in Houston, where he helped launch two tech start-ups. He then enrolled at Nashville's Vanderbilt University to pursue his MBA. Meanwhile, Bell studied film and digital animation at Hampshire College in Massachusetts before landing in New York City, where he freelanced in digital production for networks around Manhattan. After witnessing the terrorist attacks of 9/11, Darek and his wife, Amy Lee, moved back to Nashville where Bell immersed himself in his family's construction business, which he assumed control of in 2005. It was around this time that Bell and Webber reconnected.

They picked up as adults right where they left off as kids by setting up a science-based side gig. In late 2006, they created a biofuel company that retrofitted school buses to run on spent vegetable oil from school cafeteria kitchens. It seemed like a great idea at the time, but by mid-summer, when Webber was sweating bullets in a non-air-conditioned garage, elbow deep in sludgy, black grease, he said, "If that tank was filled with whiskey instead of biofuel, I would be a lot happier." Webber forgot about the remark, but Bell called a few days later and proposed they switch course and open a distillery.

Before Bell and Webber dove into biofuel, they had carefully assembled profit-and-loss analysis for different ideas, evaluated potential viability, and performed market research for half a dozen different plans. These were well-thought-out analyses built to predict maximum profit and sustainability. When Bell and Webber hit on the distillery idea, however, they did none of that; they just went for it. Bell wanted a creative outlet outside the construction business, and Webber was psyched to start something he was passionate about. Without crunching a single number, Bell and Webber resolved to create a whiskey company.

The partners began their whiskey journey by fermenting beer in Bell's 350-square-foot garage in a Nashville suburb, distilling the wash in home-made stills they built from copper piping and stainless-steel drums. As they were learning how to distill, Webber applied for the appropriate licenses and permits in 2007 and quickly hit a roadblock. Tennessee would not permit a distillery in Nashville's Davidson County or anywhere in the state reasonably convenient. It didn't help that two out of the three Tennessee counties that allowed distilling in 2007 were already occupied by behemoth whiskey producers Cascade Hollow (formerly George Dickel) and Jack Daniels. When Prohibition was rolled back, the large producers made sure they could open again in their respective counties, but they weren't concerned about anyone else. Tennessee lawmakers happily closed off distilling to the rest of the state.

Fortunately for Bell and Webber, the border of Kentucky—where the laws are a whole lot friendlier—was just a few miles north.

➤➤ABSINTHE, GIN, AND WHISKEY

Bowling Green is a vibrant university city with a rocking downtown an hour's drive from Nashville. Bell and Webber set up shop inside the basement of a historic 19th-century department store in the heart of the city's town center. The 2,000-square-foot space wasn't much, but it had high ceilings and a loading dock. Corsair incorporated in Bowling Green in January 2008 and ordered a hybrid pot-and-column still from Vendome Copper & Brass Works in Louisville. Next, they purchased an old, refurbished gin still from Bill Owens, founder of the American Distilling Institute (ADI). This was a direct steam-fired 240-gallon pot still that was found covered in rotting leaves and left for dead. It made its way to Owens, who sent the still to Vendome in Louisville before it was purchased by Webber and Bell. Corsair's first distillation was in September 2008.

To launch Corsair, Bell and Webber followed a familiar pattern of developing unaged spirits to have a saleable product while building a whiskey program. They searched for classic recipes and distilling methods for both white and brown spirits to create a baseline for their experiments. Classic recipes were surprisingly difficult to find in 2008, but they did find a collection of absinthe recipes that were recorded by prominent scholars who would visit absinthe distilleries in Europe in the late 19th century. This is why absinthe was Corsair's first product.

Then they turned their attention to gin. To prototype combinations of botanicals, Webber developed a slick desktop glass distillation system called a rotary evaporator. The wash is poured into a 500-milliliter glass "pot" container and rotated by a motor in an oil bath to maintain a constant heat transfer through the glass. It's not as consistent as copper but it produced a gin prototype in 40 minutes. One hundred and fifty recipes later, the blend of botanicals for Corsair was set. Now it was time to make American single malt.

Bell and Webber did not have the space or equipment to ferment wash in the tight Bowling Green distillery, so Webber rented time at Yazoo Brewing in Nashville, where he'd brew one of the dozen different beer recipes, then drive the wash an hour north to Bowling Green for distilling, barreling, and aging.

Being science geeks, it was natural for Bell and Webber to dive into experimenting with unique flavor combinations, then catalog their findings. These experiments fell into three categories. The first was malt barley. There are hundreds of malt variations, called adjuncts, considered by brewers, but American whiskey makers often utilize malt more to convert starch to enzymes than for its flavor. Bell and Webber, however, experimented with hundreds of adjuncts to explore each variation's impact on flavor.

The second realm of experimentation was alternative grains. Bell and Webber combined unusual ingredients like triticale and oat with a range

Making Good Whiskey in Small Barrels with Andrew Webber

The smaller the barrel, the more influence the wood has in a shorter amount of time. For this reason, craft producers will use small barrels to accelerate aging and put their whiskey on the shelf more quickly, lest they go broke waiting years for a full-sized barrel to work its magic without a return on investment. Small barrels are easier to store, more efficient, and—according to many—make better whiskey. The challenge with smaller barrels is that because there's a higher wood-to-liquid ratio, oak and tannin can easily overpower the distillate before the whiskey has time to develop the lovely caramel, vanilla, and spice flavors that barrels impart over time. This is referred to as "small barrel flavor." The reason for this is too much infusion and not enough oxidation—the two processes a barrel provides as an aging environment. Infusion is when whiskey "breathes" into and out of the toast and char layers inside a barrel and takes on more of the barrel's influence. Oxidation is when oak allows oxygen to penetrate the wood, breaking down larger molecules, removing nasty oils, and chopping up foul-tasting chemicals into smaller, tastier congeners.

Webber discovered that in order to minimize "small barrel" flavor and enhance positive congeners, you need a tighter tails cut than you would for a standard 53-gallon barrel. This removes the off-flavors that don't have time to break down through oxidation in a smaller barrel. By chopping out the molecules that hurt a young whiskey's flavor, the distiller can focus on teasing out the tastiest flavors, even in a 15- or 30-gallon barrel.

of malt variations, like roasted or raw.

Finally, they experimented with smoke. Bell and Webber loved whiskey of all shapes and sizes but especially adored the smoky, funky, heavily peated single malt scotches from distilleries that dot the coast of Islay, Scotland. But they were also aware that peat smoke is a polarizing flavor many find off-putting. Peat was a fuel source in Scotland that developed into a flavor out of tradition. In the United States, fuel sources like wood and charcoal are flavor components in barbeque and grilling. Smoke's effect on flavor in American barbeque is well documented, so Bell and Webber saw an opportunity to tap into this knowledge and apply it to distilling American whiskey. After exploring and documenting a spectrum of flavors, Bell and Webber developed their first and most popular whiskey, Triple Smoke. This malt whiskey is a blend of traditional peated scotch malt, beechwood-smoked Rausch malt from Germany, and cherrywood-smoked barley from Greece. This juice was aged in a combination of 15- and 30-gallon barrels.

➨CRAFTING THE CRAFT COMMUNITY

When Bell and Webber set up shop in Kentucky, they were surprised to be invited to join the Kentucky Distillers' Association. The KDA is predominantly a lobbying organization comprising large whiskey distillers whose agenda ensures that Kentucky remains a distilling state. In response to the mounting influx of micro-distillers, the association created a craft membership and instituted the Kentucky Bourbon Trail Craft Tour (KBTCT). This arm of KDA is dedicated to craft distillers, whose members maintain an inventory of under 10,000 barrels of Kentucky spirits annually. The craft members manage the KBTCT. Webber was invited to join the craft board, and there he found a friendly community of like-minded distillers who openly shared knowledge and best practices.

Through the KDA, Webber connected with large producers who formed the Distilled Spirits Council (DISCUS), a national trade association that lobbies in Washington, DC, for the alcohol industry. DISCUS launched a craft distilling board in 2010, which Webber was invited to join. Before becoming a founding member of the American Craft Spirits Association, Webber was also active in the American Distilling Institute.

Meanwhile, Corsair was growing in a way Bell and Webber never expected. After winning their first gold medals from the award circuit, they picked up media buzz in early 2009 for making unusual whiskey. This caught the attention of cocktail bars in Seattle who were riding the crest of a craft cocktail wave and searching for unique spirits to build drinks around. When a distributor invited Corsair to enter Washington State, Webber agreed. After becoming a cultish cocktail vehicle in Seattle, Corsair launched in Chicago, then New York. Smoky and strange, Corsair was gaining the mystique of a hip, mysterious, big city brand.

➳ BACK TO TENNESSEE

Bell and Webber launched Corsair in Bowling Green out of necessity, but their hearts remained in Nashville. They immediately set about trying to improve liquor regulatory laws in Tennessee. In the pursuit, they connected with an unlikely ally, former Tennessee legislator Mike Williams, who was interested in creating his own craft company. Williams had retired from politics but had connections and knew how to push a bill through. Corsair became the poster child for the growing craft distilling movement in Tennessee. After all, Corsair was the company forced to move to Kentucky after being turned away by Tennessee. By 2010, Bell, Webber, and Williams managed to free about half the state for distilling, including Nashville. Now Corsair could have a pot-still operation locally without having to drive the wash an hour to Bowling Green.

In a turn of good fortune, the owner of the Yazoo brewery wanted to relocate to a larger location and offered to sell their brewpub to Corsair. The brewery is located inside the Marathon Motor Works Building, a two-

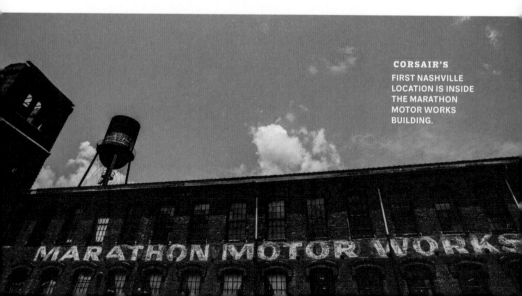

CORSAIR'S
FIRST NASHVILLE
LOCATION IS INSIDE
THE MARATHON
MOTOR WORKS
BUILDING.

block-long brick structure that was an engine plant in the late 19th century before being converted to a car factory in the early 1900s. The brewery was fully functional, with a taproom, restaurant, and 300-gallon brewer's kit. Corsair jumped at the chance, and within a few months, they were granted the required permits to move their large still to the facility. The Bowling Green location became a white spirits distillery, while whiskey production was resumed in what they now referred to as the Corsair Marathon brew-stillery. People could tour the brewery/distillery with a pint of craft beer in hand, then do a whiskey tasting at the end.

Once situated in Tennessee, Bell and Webber ramped up their whiskey pro-totype program, from which came their next two products: Ryemageddon and Corsair Moonshine. The team tested rye recipes when they cooked up the mash bill for Ryemageddon, a marriage of malted rye, barley, and malt choco-late rye. The guys loved the spirit right off the still, so they changed course and put the unaged whiskey in a bottle instead of a barrel and sold it as moonshine.

➤ THE MALT HOUSE

To double down on their commitment to studying the effects of malt on fermentation and as a flavor influencer, Bell built a malt house on his family farm outside of Nashville in 2014. He and Webber installed a floor malt system into a 5,000-square-foot metal shed, malting 1,000- to 2,000-pound batches of rye, barley, and historic grains like spelt. Next, they converted large metal containers into individual smokehouses and began smoking these grains. The shed became a grain laboratory where

CORSAIR'S

ORIGINAL WHISKEY, WHICH IS USED FOR TRIPLE SMOKE, IS MADE IN THIS PRE-PROHIBITION GIN STILL.

Bell and Webber continued their science-driven passion for recording information about their experiments. These experiments led to dozens of out-of-the-box limited-release whiskeys showcasing the findings of their research. A few examples include a "green malt" whiskey, made from un-kilned (dried) malt barley, and Hydra, a combination of barley smoked from a variety of wood: pecan, apple, sugar maple, black walnut, and persimmon.

Wood-Smoked Grains

In Scotland, the traditional fuel source to kiln moist malt barley is peat. But Bell and Webber have found that different grains absorb smoke differently. Here are four common types of smoke Corsair works with.

- **CITRUS WOOD:** A lot of the flavor in a spirit comes from oils, and citrus wood has many of the same oils found in the tree's fruit, like grapefruit, orange, and particularly lemon. These flavors transfer beautifully to the whiskey.
- **NUT WOOD:** Barley smoked with pecan wood will contribute pecan's signature nutty sweetness to the whiskey. Walnut imparts bitterness that can easily overwhelm, but if used correctly, it adds curious umami flavors that taste like you've added bitters to your whiskey.
- **GRAPE ROOT:** Grape root is an example of how smoking grains will contribute more than flavor to a whiskey. The oils in grape root contribute heavily to an unctuous, fatty mouthfeel that is similar to the effect of oils from herbs in gin.
- **HICKORY:** This is a workhorse smoke that's neither too ashy or acerbic. Hickory produces a clean smoke with familiar flavors that carry over to the whiskey to create barbeque in a glass.

⇻WEHO

By 2014, Corsair was tapped out of barrel storage space in Nashville, so it was back to shipping barrels to Bowling Green for aging. But that was a Band-Aid, not a cure. To expand, Corsair purchased a 12,000-square-foot warehouse space in WeHo, a hopping neighborhood just a few blocks south of downtown Nashville, in 2014. Then came the hardware. After bringing two 550-gallon wash stills into Marathon, Bell and Webber ordered a pair of 3,000-gallon wash stills for the WeHo spot, as well as a classic 800-gallon pot still. Between what was now three facilities, Corsair had nine stills and the ability to ramp up production to national levels.

WHY DOESN'T ANYBODY MALT CORN?

While barley is the traditional choice for malt, plenty of recipes have been surfacing that feature malted rye, wheat, and other grains. But rarely does corn enter the malt conversation. Here's why:

1. It doesn't convert starch to sugar: Corn has a stronger starch structure than rye, barley, or wheat, so you need to boil it. This deactivates the enzymes you unlocked from the malting process, which are required to break down starch to sugar so the yeast can convert it to alcohol.

2. It doesn't contribute much flavor: Malted corn tastes just like unmalted corn, therefore it's not a significant taste influencer.

3. It's a pain in the ass: Malting corn is a sloppy process, and bacteria problems are common.

The following year, Webber's experience with KDA helped shape what became the Tennessee Distillers Guild, which Bell and Webber participated in founding. To everyone's surprise, the large distilleries like Jack Daniels and George Dickel supported upstart entrepreneurs, helping to create an inclusive community fighting for fair laws that make it possible to flourish in the industry.

By 2017, Corsair had twenty to thirty different limited-edition bottlings and seasonal releases, like a fall pumpkin ale and a springtime green malt whiskey. For Webber, it was great to be creative, but by 2017, sales distributors were fed up with all the whiskeys in their warehouse. This was the downside of Corsair throwing spaghetti on the wall to see what sticks. In bars, Corsair's salespeople pushed to find a sacred spot on cocktail lists, then the limited-run whiskey would run out of stock and be discontinued. So Bell and Webber focused on pumping out core products and letting several of their annual releases fall away.

Corsair closed the Bowling Green location in 2018 and moved the white spirits program to WeHo, finally consolidating in Nashville. At the time of writing, the team has ordered a column still, meaning bourbon may be on the horizon. But knowing Corsair, it's doubtful it will be done the way Jack, George, or the boys in Kentucky do it.

What's in the Bottle?
Corsair Triple Smoke

THE VITALS: 100% malted barley; NAS; 40% ABV (80 proof); non-chill-filtered.

PROCESS: Triple Smoke is an American single malt that has three malt flavors. (The rules state that a single malt is derived from one distillery, not from one malt.) This whiskey is a marriage of peated Scotch malt, German beechwood-smoked Rausch malt, and cherrywood-smoked barley from the US, which brings in sweet barbeque flavors. The wash is made by lautering the mash, meaning the liquid is separated from the solids in the mash. This is called distilling "off the grain." The liquid is fermented 3–5 days, then undergoes a two-pass distillation. Head, heart, and tail cuts are tighter than typical American whiskey. The hearts enter a #3 or #4 new charred oak American barrel ranging from 15–53 gallons in size.

TASTE: A smoky, peaty, fruity nose gives way to cherry and menthol on the palate with an accompaniment of smoke that follows through on the finish, where it mingles with malt and sweetness.

SOUTHERN HOSPITALITY

Whiskey distilleries have popped up all over the United States, and the South is no exception. Here are a few that are making beautiful whiskey in unexpected places.

Rock Town, Little Rock, AR

ESTABLISHED: 2010

THE WHISKEYS: Arkansas Bourbon; Four Grain Sour Mash Straight Bourbon; Bottled-in-Bond Bourbon; Straight Rye; Straight Barley Bourbon; Straight Golden Promise Bourbon; Straight Chocolate Malt Bourbon; Hickory Smoked Whiskey

THE STORY: When the craft distilling scene started gathering steam in 2009, Phil Brandon found himself wondering why the hell there weren't any distilleries in Arkansas. The state has great water and locally grown grain, and Little Rock sits on the same latitude as Jack Daniels, 400 miles to the east. One year later, Rock Town was born. Paving the way for other Arkansas distillers, in 2011 Brandon worked to change the law to allow distilleries to sell their spirits by the bottle. In 2017, he returned to the legislature to successfully lobby to allow distillers to sell by the drink. Afterward, Brandon moved from his East Little Rock warehouse to a larger space in SoMa, a funky neighborhood on south Main Street where he built a distillery, tasting room, rickhouse, and cocktail bar. In the distillery, locally grown corn, rye, and wheat (barley is not currently grown in Arkansas) are used to make the core lineup of Rock Town's signature and Four Grain bourbons as well as their Straight Rye. Brandon's penchant for mash-bill tinkering has led to the development of his Flavor Grain Series, which explores various grain types, malts, and smoke.

St. Augustine Distillery, St. Augustine, FL

ESTABLISHED: 2013

THE WHISKEYS: Florida Straight Bourbon; Port Finished Bourbon; The Saint Bourbon

THE STORY: When proprietors Mike Diaz and Phil McDaniel constructed St. Augustine Distillery in a historic ice factory in northeast Florida in 2013, they focused on visitor experience over wide distribution at first. The strategy paid off. In 2019, this little-known distillery had visitor numbers that rivalled Maker's Mark's. Visitors browsed the gift shop, taking home giftable, house-made vodkas, gins, and rums while St. Augustine's whiskey stocks matured. To develop their whiskey program, Diaz and McDaniel tapped former Maker's Mark head distiller Dave Pickerell for their equipment design and Stranahan's head distiller Jake Norris for their bourbon recipe. Norris's bourbon mash is a recipe of Florida-grown grains: 60 percent corn, 22 percent barley, and 18 percent winter wheat. It is double pot distilled before entering a 53-gallon barrel where maturation and blending are managed in consultation with expert Nancy Fraley of Nosing Services, then bottled at no less than three years old.

High Wire Distilling, Charleston, SC

ESTABLISHED: 2010

THE WHISKEYS: New Southern Revival Sorghum Whiskey; New Southern Revival Rye

THE STORY: High Wire is an agriculturally focused distillery founded by Scott Blackwell and his wife, Ann, in Charleston, South Carolina. High Wire's credo is to let the grain do the talking. This philosophy led Blackwell down a deep rabbit hole of exploring funky grain strains that have become the cornerstone of High Wire's portfolio. Blackwell's first release was a sorghum whiskey, a grain he had used in gluten-free products when he owned a commercial baking company in his former life. While his sorghum whiskey barrels were maturing, Blackwell collaborated with Glenn Roberts of Anson Mills in Charleston to grow Jimmy Red, a corn from St. James Island, which locals coined "hooch corn." The 100 percent corn bourbon has a honey sweetness backed up by a spice that experts swear could only come from rye or wheat. High Wire rye is made from Abruzzi, a puny-looking rye strain with colonial roots. After testing the grain from five different areas in the country, the wild flux in flavors convinced Blackwell that terroir does indeed exist in whiskey.

ST. AUGUSTINE'S RENOVATION OF AN OLD ICE FACTORY WON TWO HISTORICAL PRESERVATION AWARDS IN THE CITY.

CHAPTER 8

KINGS COUNTY

HOW
COLIN SPOELMAN
MADE HIS
"SHINER" SPIRIT
FROM THE
APPALACHIAN HILLS
THE BACKBONE
OF A BIG CITY
DISTILLERY

THE DISTILLERY: Kings County
ESTABLISHED: 2010
LOCATION: Brooklyn, NY
THE WHISKEYS: Moonshine; Chocolate Whiskey; Kings County Bourbon; Peated Single Malt; Peated Bourbon; Bourbon Bottled-in-Bond; Empire Rye; Winter Spice Whiskey
WHY KINGS COUNTY MATTERS: When best-selling author and *New York Times* editor Clay Risen declared in the *Atlantic Monthly* that "If it's sold on liquor-store shelves, it's not moonshine," he was technically incorrect. Moonshine is permissible as a "fanciful term" in the United States, meaning there are no rules preventing producers from labeling products as such. But everyone knows what Risen meant. The term refers to illegal liquor, and anything that calls itself otherwise is considered a poser. But Colin Spoelman argues that moonshine is whatever an Appalachian says it is. The culture he grew up in wasn't focused on legality. The "shine" Spoelman knew was rooted in respect for the craft and pride in making something well. If that's not what Spoelman's doing with his perfectly legal "white whiskey" moonshine, he concedes not to know what the real thing is.

➤ WHITE LIGHTNING

The northern part of central Kentucky, between Louisville and Lexington, has long been ruled by the well-heeled, fancy-hat-wearing, thoroughbred-obsessed bourbon elite. But Kings County Distillery cofounder Colin Spoelman grew up in a whole different Kentucky. Due east of the pristine bourbon distilleries and over-the-top visitor centers is Appalachia, a rugged region festooned with canyons, ridge tops, and rock cliffs. Tucked in these hills exists a hard-core American values culture embracing sustainable farming, folk art, and a local and not wholly legal moonshine distilling tradition.

Spoelman grew up in Harlan City in the heart of Kentucky's Appalachia region. Growing up in this "dry" town did not mean the town was actually dry. It was quite the opposite. The area's historical tradition of

illegal distilling sprung from its local political conditions and geographic isolation; the local cops were either in on it or cool with it, and distillers lived too remotely for people to check on them often. Harlan is inside Harlan County, the setting for the classic film *Thunder Road*, where Robert Mitchum's character is a moon-runner, doing his best not to be arrested by the cops or murdered by gangsters while delivering high-proofed white lightning. Back in the day, those cat-and-mouse games were quite real. But the illegal booze scene that Spoelman grew up around in the 1990s wasn't so dramatic.

There were two types of illegal alcohol purveyors in Harlan when Spoelman was a teen: moonshiners and bootleggers. "Moonshine" is slang term for an illegally produced distilled spirit. A moonshiner is the distiller making said moonshine. In Appalachia, moonshine was usually a recipe of corn (for flavor) and sugar (for alcohol), bottled unaged at whatever proof its maker deemed appropriate. But the stuff was usually quite strong. A bootlegger was an illegal store, usually in someone's home, where you would buy commercial alcohol and beer at a slight markup. Illegal shine was also usually available. The bonus for a kid like Spoelman? Bootleggers never checked IDs.

After high school, Spoelman migrated east to study architecture and theater at Yale University in Connecticut. He landed in Brooklyn after graduation, where he worked for an academic architect who designed international campus museum installations. When Spoelman visited family in Kentucky, he made sure to bring a little backwoods hooch home to Brooklyn. The authentic mountain shine was always fun to pass around at parties. Spoelman would educate the food-obsessed, intellectual city crowd about a Kentucky distilling tradition that had been around since Germans and Scots settled in the mountainous terrain during the 1700s to purposely remain isolated and avoid the government.

To Spoelman, there's a romance to this longstanding craft distilling tradition. He argues that while corporate bourbon companies try to convince you they still have authentic, small-batch whiskey, they don't. The ones who have been making true handmade craft hooch all along are the moonshiners, not the bourbon makers. To produce the delicious, unaged, Appalachian shine, illegal distillers produce small batches of the highest quality distillate they can muster, often under compromised conditions, and without the hardware and resources of a commercial distillery. Nor do shiners rely on barrels to sort out the whiskey. What comes off the still

A Ridiculously Brief History of
Moonshine

The business of running moonshine started around the Civil War when an excise tax was levied on alcohol to help fund the war. Scot, German, and Irish immigrant distillers fled the revenue officers in major cities like Philadelphia, New York, and Baltimore and relocated to remote locations where they were free to distill without paying a tax. For obvious reasons, the moonshine trade hit a fevered pitch during Prohibition. But when the 18th Amendment was repealed by the 21st Amendment in 1933, several states like North Carolina, Mississippi, and Tennessee stayed dry for years. They became prime locales for a moonshine cottage industry.

Moonshining used to be a game of profit, but things have changed. The federal excise tax on alcohol has held steady at $13.50 per proof gallon for decades. Meanwhile, inflation has risen so much that what was once a massive burden on distillers and a fat profit margin for moonshiners in the 1950s and '60s has dwindled down to the point where it's not worth the risk of jail time. For this reason, may old-time ex-moonshiners are today's bootleggers, or occasionally legal distillers. Today's shiners are usually hobbyists, even if they are dead serious about their liquor.

is what you drink: the result of your ingredients, conditions, and talent.

Spoelman recognized that moonshine fit perfectly with the growing farm-to-table ethos. Inspired to make his own shine, he purchased an eight-gallon still off the internet in 2008

⇒SHINE BOYS

Distilling illegally in Spoelman's Brooklyn apartment was purely a hobby at first. He realized during the earliest experiments that it's not necessary to have fancy tech degrees or a family distilling lineage to make a clean distillate that, in his opinion, stands up to the legal stuff on the market. During this time, Spoelman reunited with his college roommate, David Haskell, who came to New York to pursue a journalism career. Spoelman moved into Haskell's East Williamsburg apartment, where the friends began distilling together. Eventually they decided to make their illegal operation legit. After scraping together funds from friends and family, the partners rented a tiny commercial space on Meadow Street in Williamsburg, teetering on the edge of Bushwick, and applied for permits. On April 14, 2010, Kings County obtained the first New York City distiller's license in almost a century.

The original distillery was a tiny 250-square-foot studio with no air-conditioning in a funky building that housed several small recording studios, indie magazines, and a beef jerky company. Inside this little space, they installed five eight-gallon pot stills that required two full-time shifts to produce three gallons of white dog each day. The distillate—made from New York-grown corn and English malt—was either bottled as moonshine or dumped into five-gallon oak barrels to make bourbon. Spoelman split time between his architecture job and the distillery. Haskell had a full-time position at *New York Magazine*. Help was needed to manage the maturation program for their growing collection of aging barrels.

➤➤A STAR IS BORN

Spoelman and Haskell sold their first case of moonshine on August 1, 2010. The big launch was a tasting session at Uva Wine in Williamsburg, since they were not yet permitted to pour samples at their distillery. On this fateful day, a young chemical engineer named Nicole Austin showed up at Uva and introduced herself. Austin lived in Cobble Hill, Brooklyn, working for an environmental engineering firm and hanging out at Char No. 4, one of the great Brooklyn craft whiskey bars. It was here that Austin fell in love with whiskey and craft distilling. One day she had an epiphany. As a chemical engineer, Austin realized she already knew how to distill fuel types and pharmaceuticals, the same process as producing alcohol. Austin scoured distillery events and whiskey festivals, making contacts and putting herself out there. After Austin discovered Kings County was opening shop in her city, she made sure to be on the scene that day at Uva and made it clear that the guys needed her. And they agreed. Austin's whiskey career was underway.

➤➤TRAGICALLY HIP

It was an exciting time to sell whiskey in Williamsburg, the hipster capital of the world. The location brought an instant cool factor, especially with a handful of hip cocktail bars making waves around the city. It's accepted as common knowledge that the handcrafted cocktail movement that swept

KINGS
COUNTY'S
BAR AND
TASTING ROOM

spirit-woke places like Brooklyn during this time was a critical factor in the rise of craft spirits.

Char No. 4, Normans Kill, Maysville, and Brandy Library were a few early supporters who put Kings County liquid in cocktails. Still, Spoelman found the bartenders in his backyard incredibly dismissive of anything made outside Kentucky. To acquire fans, Kings County went directly to customers through tastings and expos, which they hoped would pressure more bars to carry their liquor. It was a slog for other small producers, too, which led to independent producers banding together. Meanwhile, Spoelman was facing another challenge: Kings County had a hipster problem.

The year 2010 was an unusual moment in Brooklyn culture. E-commerce and social media were advanced enough that people could launch and promote small-scale businesses in ways they never could before. Williamsburg was an incubator for these artisan companies, especially in the culinary sector, as the local-and-sustainable food movement tightened its

grip on New York City. Suddenly, specialized companies popped up like organic popcorn: mustard shops, pickle purveyors, and coffee importers...the list was endless. Spoelman felt like this movement was rooted in lifestyle, not a passion for craft.

➤ A MELTING POT

After Balcones released Brimstone and Corsair struck gold with Triple Smoke, Spoelman noticed a lot of aggressively smoked whiskeys being released in their wake. He created a smoky yet peated single malt that Kings County hoped would appeal to the blended-scotch drinker. Kings County Peated Bourbon is the product that would come to symbolize what, in Spoelman's view, Kings County is all about. The whiskey's origins were one of those happy accidents you hear about so often in the whiskey business: One fateful day the distillery ran out of malt barley for their bourbon mash, but they had peated barley left over from a recent single malt whiskey run. So with Spoelman's blessing, distiller Rob Easter tried a bourbon

KINGS COUNTY DISTILLERY
peated bourbon
bourbon whiskey
45% alcohol by volume, 750ml

What's in the Bottle? Kings County Peated Bourbon

THE VITALS: Age-stated-one-year; 45% ABV/90 proof; 75% corn and 25% peated Scottish malt; non-chill-filtered.

PROCESS: Based on Appalachia's moonshine culture, Kings County's style has evolved to sit somewhere between American bourbon (corn, rye, and new oak barrels) and a scotch blend (pot distillation, peated malt, marrying styles). A mash of 75% New York-grown corn and 25% lightly peated barley is cooked and then open fermented in wood and steel. This distiller's beer is fed into a 1,300-gallon stripping still for the first distillation, then enters one of two 260-gallon Forsyth pot stills for the second run. The whiskey released so far has been aged in 15-gallon barrels, but bourbon in 30- and 53-gallon barrels is resting.

TASTE: This Peated Bourbon is not a peat bomb like Lagavulin or Laphraoig from Islay. The peated barley is a medium-low peat and comprises only 25% of the recipe, which explains why it doesn't overpower the spirit, but instead becomes interwoven with accompanying flavors like grain, chocolate, and leather.

KINGS COUNTY HARDWARE: THE STRIPPING STILL (*LEFT*) IS 1,350 GALLONS; THE SPIRIT STILLS (*RIGHT*) ARE 265 AND 172 GALLONS.

made of corn and the smoky malt. The result was a lovely distillate with a sweet, clean smoke that blew Spoelman away. They immediately began laying down barrels. For Spoelman, this whiskey was a fusion of Scotch and American styles made right in New York, one of the world's most diverse cities, setting Kings County apart from what was going on in Louisville, Indiana, or Scotland.

The next whiskey laid down was a Bottled-in-Bond bourbon, and this one was no accident. The craft whiskey landscape was becoming crowded in 2012. As more competition filled the space, distillers like Kings County suddenly found themselves competing with well-disguised, Brooklyn-based whiskey companies sourcing their products from commercial distillers in the South or Midwest. Even New York senator Chuck Schumer was embarrassed when he praised a "New York" bourbon that was distilled in the Midwest. Kings County decided to produce a Bottled-in-Bond whiskey to squash any questions about the origins of their whiskey. (Bottled-in-Bond is a 125-year-old statement of rules requiring a whiskey be distilled by one distiller, at one distillery, in one season. It demonstrates the authenticity whiskey drinkers love about American whiskey.)

It only took a couple of years for Kings County to outgrow the Meadow Street distillery in Williamsburg. The partners relocated to the Brooklyn Navy Yards, a massive, defunct shipyard on the East River in northwest Brooklyn. This was a fresh beginning for the partners, who were able to shake the hipster funk and have a home with enough space to grow. Spoelman installed five 26-gallon moonshine stills, then ordered a pair of custom 1,000- and 650-liter Forsyth pot stills from Scotland. Demand for stills was off the charts in 2013, and it took about two and a half years for the Forsyth stills to arrive. After settling in the new space, Spoelman scaled back his architecture work and finally paid himself a salary to focus on distilling full-time.

➽ NEW YORK STATE OF MIND

Back at Kings County, Nicole Austin took charge of maturation and blending, and her contribution to Kings County's product development cannot be understated. Austin's ability to speak eloquently about moonshine culture as well as the technical side of distilling proved important in educating, promoting, and selling product.

Austin soon became a leader within the craft industry, as well. When Ralph Erenzo called a meeting at Tuthilltown in 2013 to discuss developing what became the New York State Distillers Guild, Austin was in attendance. It was Austin who hired the attorney who registered the NYSDG as a nonprofit to get the ball rolling. After a board structure was decided, formal elections were held. Austin was named president. Now this group of independent producers had strength in numbers to modernize distillery laws, and they came to Albany with the collective ability to create significant jobs, boost local agriculture, and promote tourism. (And make some fine hooch.)

One of the less tangible but extremely important benefits to the NYSDG forging relationships with Albany's legislators was a shift in attitude. When Erenzo first began working with the state in 2003, the State Liquor Authority told him it viewed distillers as legal drug dealers and would treat them accordingly. However, thanks to the groundwork laid by Austin, Erenzo, and the rest of the guild, relations improved. Governor Andrew Cuomo instituted a craft distillers' arm for Empire State Business Development. What began as a contentious relationship evolved into one where at least the State Liquor Authority and the New York alcoholic beverage industry are on the same page: Valuable businesses deserve to realize their potential.

While Nicole Austin was working to improve New York's spirits regulations, Spoelman and Haskell were busy improving Kings County back at the Navy Yards. The Forsyth stills they had ordered in 2012 were finally ready near the end of 2014, and the company could now scale up to competitive levels—by craft standards, anyway. But by then, the team realized that in order to compete in the expanding whiskey market, they had to increase production by ten times within five years. Spoelman and Haskell don't want to be the next Grey Goose, but they don't intend to settle as a New York micro-distillery either. The sweet spot is a national presence in specialty and boutique stores, as well as adventurous whiskey bars. When a 1,300-gallon stripping still arrived in 2018, Kings County was primed to take their national presence to the next level.

➥QUEEN OF EMPIRE RYE

The next project for Kings County began in 2015 when Nicole Austin returned from an ACSA convention in Denver with newfound determination to develop what became Empire Rye. Spoelman played around with rye when first starting but found it impossible to produce it cost-effectively with the old setup in Williamsburg. But Austin was equipped with a recipe and a plan, and she wasn't taking no for an answer. Besides, the upgraded equipment was better suited to producing rye. The team made about a hundred cases to see how it would go.

By this point, New York–based rye producers were popping up all over the state. Rye had enjoyed a rich distilling tradition in the state prior to Prohibition, so producers saw value in establishing a provenance to New York rye. Chris Williams from Coppersea Distilling called together a tight

group of New York–based distillers, including Austin, to establish a consortium dedicated to establishing a designation around the usage of the Empire Rye logo. The group threw a big party for fellow rye producers after Empire Rye received a title to launch the initiative. Governor Cuomo even announced a New York Rye Week.

Empire Rye Standards of Identity

The six original members agreed upon this set of rules that a distiller must adhere to in order to label their whiskey Empire Rye. Founders include Colin Spoelman and Nicole Austin of Kings County Distillery; Ralph Erenzo of Tuthilltown Spirits; Christopher Williams of Coppersea Distilling; Allen Katz and Bill Potter of New York Distilling Company; Brian McKenzie of Finger Lakes Distilling; and Jason Barrett of Black Button Distilling.

- Must conform to the New York Farm Distiller (Class D) requirement that 75% of the mash bill be New York grain.
- The remaining 25% of the mash bill may be composed of any raw or malted grain, New York–grown or otherwise, or any combination thereof.
- Distilled to no more than 160 proof.
- Aged for a minimum of two years in charred, new oak barrels at not more than 115 proof at time of entry.
- Must be mashed, fermented, distilled, barreled, and aged at a single New York State distillery.
- A blended whiskey containing no less than 100% qualifying Empire Rye whiskeys from multiple distilleries may be called Blended Empire Rye.

➤AUSTIN OUT

Empire Rye was Austin's last major project for Kings County. In 2016, she was hired as a commissioning engineer at Tullamore DEW in Ireland. After her two-year contract expired, Austin returned to the States, where she was named master distiller of Cascade Hollow, aka George Dickel, the Tennessee whiskey collection owned by Diageo, one of the world's largest spirits companies.

When Austin departed Kings County, the blending program was assumed by longtime employee Ryan Ciuchta. Austin's responsibilities within the distilling community fell to Spoelman. While Spoelman had originally been a skeptic of the Empire Rye program, he grew to become one of its biggest supporters. Spoelman appreciated how the initiative brought distillers together not because of politics but because of a product of which they were all proud. This was something easy to get behind. Empire Rye launched in 2017 and was a runaway hit for all involved.

⇥⇥TODAY, TOMORROW, AND 10 YEARS FROM NOW

For the past decade, Kings County has built a reputation for releasing whiskey based on taste, not age. In fact, Spoelman thinks basing buying decisions on price or age statement alone is missing the point; spirits should be judged on merit and free of preconceptions. But Spoelman is also aware that well-aged whiskey is delicious, and since 2013 he has been quietly maturing barrels meant to age for as long as 12 years. These mature barrels are the building blocks for the future of Kings County's whiskey program, which will always be based on the bedrock of Appalachian moonshine culture.

OAK MAGIC: FIFTEEN-GALLON BARRELS AT REST. BARREL #100, LAST ON THE LEFT IN THE FOREGROUND, CONTAINS KINGS COUNTY'S OLDEST STOCK, AT 9.5 YEARS OLD AS OF 2020.

WIDOW JANE'S
LISA WICKER

BROOKLYN GOES BIG TIME

A Spotlight on Widow Jane

WIDOW JANE'S PRESIDENT, head distiller, and head blender Lisa Wicker was awfully busy when I caught up with her on the phone, mid-pandemic, in 2020. After releasing a 15-year-old bourbon that's finished in 5-year-old air-seasoned Appalachian oak, Wicker will be blending the third bottling of Widow Jane Decadence, a bourbon that's rebarreled in maple syrup casks from Crown Maple in New York's Hudson Valley. Then, Wicker's next project will be Lucky Thirteen, an age-stated single barrel bourbon sourced from MGP in Indiana.

Clearly, Widow Jane is in a good place right now. So good, in fact, that Wicker doesn't seem quite sure how things turned out this way. But anybody in the know attests that the reason the company is buzzing along so nicely is Wicker herself.

Wicker's blending skills were developed during her 10 years as a winemaker before crossing the bridge to distilling in 2011 when she learned the trade alongside Steve Beam at Limestone Branch Distillery in Lebanon, Kentucky. Four years later, Wicker was distilling at Starlight Distillery when she was invited to visit George Washington's Mount Vernon Distillery in Virginia. Her visit led to her becoming the Senior Consulting Distiller at Mount Vernon. Through this connection, Wicker was recommended by an industry insider to Samson & Surrey owners Juan Rovira and Robert Furniss-Roe, who were hunting for a director of whiskey operations. The partners had big ideas and needed a very particular somebody to shepherd the company toward its goals. Lisa got the job.

Widow Jane has always been a two-track whiskey company—distilling and blending—but

THE CACAO PRIETO BUILDING, WIDOW JANE'S DISTILLERY IN RED HOOK, BROOKLYN

it's best known for its sourced and blended bourbons and ryes. The company launched at a gratuitous time in 2012 as Widow Jane caught the crest of a mounting wave of obsession over premium American whiskey. Its signature bourbon started as a 10-year-old single barrel bottling sourced from distilleries in Kentucky and Indiana. Today the whiskey is bottled in tight, five-barrel batches. Once blended, Widow Jane whiskeys are cut, or proofed, with New York water sourced from the Rosendale Mines located 90 miles north of Brooklyn.

When Wicker arrived, she inherited an heirloom corn project. After a few seasons of experimenting with different grains, the company settled on a cross between two corn strains: Bloody Butcher, a red heirloom grain, and Wapsie Valley, a yellow-orange corn that's emerging in the culinary world. The project is growing into a major part of Widow Jane's story, and as of 2020, it's the largest heirloom corn crop for whiskey in the United States. The offspring is Baby Jane, which is currently released as a one-year bottling, though the plan is to age some out for future releases.

Most people aren't even aware that Widow Jane distills their own whiskey. But in fairness, their Brooklyn-distilled whiskeys are made in tiny batches and are only available on-site. This is about to change, though. Under Wicker's direction, plans were drawn in 2019 to begin construction on a new distillery, right up the road from the original location in Red Hook, Brooklyn. The COVID-19 shutdown sidelined construction in 2020, but since 2018 Wicker has been distilling Widow Jane part-time at Castle & Key Distillery in Kentucky, where she's been laying down thousands of barrels of bourbon and rye.

At the end of the day, though, blending will always be a huge part of Widow Jane, which in Wicker's opinion is the most challenging part of whiskey making and the part of the job she loves most. "Blending is about taking batches of good whiskey to create a beautiful whiskey," she says. "It is a challenge, but not without reward."

WIDOW JANE WHISKEYS: Widow Jane Aged 10 Years; Decadence; 12-Year-Old; Lucky Thirteen; The Vaults; American Oak Aged Rye; Apple Wood Aged Rye; Baby Jane Bourbon; Bloody Butcher Bourbon; Wapsie Valley Bourbon; Chocolate Malt Bourbon; Hopi Blue Bourbon

CHAPTER 9

SAGAMORE SPIRIT

HOW A BALTIMORE DISTILLERY IS RESTORING MARYLAND'S ONCE-PROUD RYE DISTILLING TRADITION

THE DISTILLERY: Sagamore Spirit
ESTABLISHED: 2012
LOCATION: Baltimore, Maryland
THE WHISKEYS: Straight Rye; Cask Strength Straight Rye; Double Oak Rye; Cognac Finish; Rye Ale Finish; Calvados Finish; Port Finish; Vintner's Finish; Tequila Finish
WHY SAGAMORE MATTERS: There was a time before Prohibition when rye from the mid-Atlantic states, especially Maryland and Pennsylvania, was as ubiquitous as Kentucky bourbon. Today, Sagamore Spirit is restoring a 300-year-old Maryland rye distilling tradition with a plan that supports local farming and invests in Baltimore by erecting a community distillery with the capacity to become a global brand.

⇥MARYLAND'S RYE WHISKEY HISTORY

The rye whiskey history of the mid-Atlantic states dates back to the 18th century. In the early 1700s colonists' spirit of choice was rum, the ingredients for which were imported from the English-controlled West Indies. Obviously, colonists were not on the best terms with the British in the decades leading up to the Revolutionary War, the primary source of tension being tariffs and taxes. Things came to a head when England foisted the Molasses Tax on settlers (molasses is the primary ingredient in rum production). It was time for the US to find a new spirit of choice.

Rye was a common cover crop for tobacco fields so it makes sense that farmers would distill it. Even George Washington distilled rye at his Mount Vernon home in Virginia after the Revolutionary War. Meanwhile, Scottish, Irish, and Swedish immigrants—people who know how to distill grains—were migrating to the New World. Rye whiskey soon became a mid-Atlantic staple, particularly in Maryland and Pennsylvania, and it remained that way for almost 160 years until Prohibition hobbled the industry and World War II knocked it out.

In 1910, Maryland had 44 licensed distilleries, 22 of which were in down-

MID-ATLANTIC
RENAISSANCE:
COMPANIES LIKE
SAGAMORE SPIRIT
ARE PUTTING
MARYLAND RYE BACK
IN BUSINESS.

town Baltimore. When Prohibition became law in 1919, Maryland was the only state that did not ratify the 18th Amendment, meaning lawmakers refused to pass a state enforcement act. By 1939, Maryland held one-third of the nation's rye whiskey supply—110 million gallons. When the US entered World War II, though, all working distilleries in the state were converted to ethanol plants to support the war effort. (Half of the government's 550-million-gallon ethanol quota was supplied by the beverage distilling industry.) After the war, very few of those ethanol plants converted back to rye whiskey distilleries, and Maryland rye almost disappeared. Of the few Maryland distilleries to survive, the last was Pikesville Rye, which closed in 1982. (Heaven Hill bought the brand and made the whiskey at its Bernheim Distillery in Kentucky until 2016.)

Now, however, Maryland has 25 licensed distilleries, with at least 11 producing rye whiskey. And no distillery is doing as much to return Maryland rye to its former glory as Sagamore Spirit.

⇥ THE RYE PROJECT

The history of Sagamore Spirit begins as any good whiskey story should: around a campfire. It was 2010 when soon-to-be founders Kevin Plank and Bill McDermond enjoyed a summer's evening at Plank's Sagamore Farm, a thoroughbred horse-breeding farm located 22 miles north of downtown Baltimore. From the manor's front porch, Plank looked out over the expansive fields with whiskey in hand and discussed his neighbor's suggestion that he plant a vineyard at the farm. It was a fine idea. Building a winery outside of Baltimore would create jobs and draw tourism. But Plank looked at McDermond and said, "We're whiskey guys, Billy." It didn't take much digging on McDermond's part to uncover Maryland's lost rye tradition. Once they realized they were in a position to revitalize a lost industry, they were committed.

Long before Sagamore, Plank founded Under Armour, a Baltimore-based Fortune 500 sports apparel company with over 14,500 employees. Plank started the company while playing football at the University of Maryland, where he developed sweat-wicking sports gear that he grew into a $7.8 billion corporation. Bill McDermond is Plank's business partner and was one of Under Armor's first employees.

McDermond spent two years getting the rye project off the ground, which included hiring a hydrobiologist to study the spring water at Sagamore Farm. The water tested as pure, limestone-filtered water. This is significant because this is the type of water that Kentucky bourbon makers

A RYE GUY:
BRIAN TREACY,
AGING ALONGSIDE
SAGAMORE'S
BARRELS

How Maryland Rye Gave Rise to Kentucky Bourbon

After the Revolutionary War, the nation began its independence $54 million in the hole. In 1791, Alexander Hamilton and his crew decided to pay down debt by throwing an excise tax onto alcoholic products. This was the first tax imposed on a domestic product by the new federal government. Early settlers took umbrage with this, and an exodus ensued. Tax-dodging, mid-Atlantic Maryland distilling families, Jacob Beam evidently among them, went south. Landing in what became Kentucky, these tax-dodging new settlers joined established distillers like Evan Williams and Jacob Spears in creating what became a bourbon empire. Those who stayed raised holy hell over the whole thing, sending collectors packing, sometimes tarred and feathered. Things came to a head in western Pennsylvania when organized mobs attacked a wealthy tax collector, General John Neville, and burned his home. George Washington, a rye producer himself who opposed the tax from the outset, dispatched 12,000 militiamen to cool things off. This was known as the Whiskey Rebellion. President Thomas Jefferson rescinded the tax in 1802, which kicked off a golden age of distilling in the mid-Atlantic and Midwestern states.

claim makes their whiskey special.

McDermond hired Dave Pickerell to develop the whiskey program and design the distillery. Pickerell's plan was similar to what he did at WhistlePig: source whiskey, this time from MGP in Indiana, to get the company rolling while building a facility where they could distill their own rye. The original location for Sagamore was a nondescript warehouse-style space on West Dickman Street in the Locust Point neighborhood of Baltimore. With 7,613 square feet, the garage could comfortably house a medium-sized distillery. But as Plank and McDermond moved forward, they transitioned from their business model of a boutique high-end whiskey business to wanting to go big and take on major players like Jack Daniels. To make this happen, they needed someone to run the day-to-day operations.

Entrepreneur Brian Treacy was the CEO of a successful adventure travel company when his phone rang at 7 am on a Tuesday morning. His high school buddy, Kevin Plank, was on the line. "Brian, here's the deal," Plank said. "We're launching a distillery. Bill has been working on it for a couple of years, and it's time to start growing it. I'd like you to move back to Maryland to run this thing." This was possibly the last call on the planet Treacy was expecting. The only thing he knew about whiskey was how to drink it. But Plank insisted that Treacy was the man for the job. Treacy happened to be flying back to his hometown of Baltimore for a wedding in a couple of weeks. He said he'd be happy to talk it over then. But Plank wanted him right away. Treacy found himself on a plane to Baltimore that Friday.

Bill McDermond drove Treacy from the airport to Sagamore Farm for a meeting. The business plan was simple: Make superb rye whiskey with mass appeal. It was how they planned to sell it that was distinct. McDermond recognized that most notable whiskey brands focused on older white men as the target audience, neglecting a huge section of younger, urban, and female drinkers. Kevin and Bill were passionate about introducing their spirit to a bigger crowd. And if they could do this successfully, it would have a positive impact on the Baltimore community by creating jobs and bringing awareness to the city.

Treacy returned to Arizona, sold his beloved adventure backpacking business, and moved himself and his family to Maryland. He was the new president of Sagamore Spirit.

THE CAMPUS: SAGAMORE SPIRIT HAS EVOLVED FROM A 500-GALLON POT STILL TO A WHISKEY LOVER'S PARADISE.

⇥HELP ON THE WAY

By this point, Dave Pickerell was splitting his time between WhistlePig, Hillrock, and over 100 other projects of various sizes. Truth was, he didn't have the bandwidth to give Treacy the help necessary to launch the brand. The two guys developed a keen friendship in their months working together, but ultimately they parted ways. Treacy teamed up with Larry Ebersold, the legendary former master distiller of MGP who is known in the industry as the "Godfather of Rye." Ebersold was the guy who would finally make Sagamore Spirit a reality.

It was July 9, 2013, when Treacy, McDermond, and Ebersold met up at the Jim Beam distillery in Frankfort and spent two days touring sprawling bourbon distilleries dotting Kentucky's countryside. Treacy soaked in the lifetime of knowledge that Ebersold imparted about whiskey making as they rolled past the endless horse farms on back roads between Louisville and Lexington. Treacy ogled the multimillion-dollar visitor centers at the major distilleries and the slick distillery "experiences" complete with restaurants and tasting rooms that were popping up in Louisville. As he browsed the luxe gift shop at Buffalo Trace, Treacy thought back to Sagamore's warehouse space on West Dickman and knew he needed to do better. He came back to Baltimore with a plan to turn a local curiosity into a world-class brand.

⇥RECONSTRUCTING MARYLAND RYE

Around the same time that they were pitching Plank and McDermond to upgrade their space, Treacy and Ebersold sat down to design a whiskey they felt would best represent the spirit of Maryland rye, whatever that meant. Evidence of how Maryland producers made rye in the 19th and early 20th centuries is scarce, and there are theories about why this is. Many distillers were whiskey rectifiers in the 19th century, not artisanal producers, and they avoided making records of the questionable additives commonly used to flavor whiskey. Another theory is that records that did exist were lost in the Great Baltimore Fire of 1904, a blaze that ravaged 1,500 buildings and damaged another thousand. One thing most experts agree on is that Maryland rye was known for a rounder, sweeter flavor than spicy in-your-face Pennsylvania- or Virginia-made rye. So round and sweet was what Ebersold and Treacy had to work with in developing Sagamore's product.

At Ebersold's suggestion, the team moved away from sourcing whiskey from MGP to contract distilling. There is a distinction: Sourcing means purchasing pre-made whiskey off the shelf and bottling it under your own label, while a contract model means the distillery custom distills alcohol exclusively for you. The advantage to the latter is having more control over your product—for example, stipulating when the whiskey is made (it's best to avoid distilling in the summer), adjusting proof, and sourcing your own grain. It didn't hurt that Ebersold was revered like Jesus at MGP, so chances were that projects with his name attached would be treated as top-notch.

The disadvantage to contract distilling is that when the whiskey is made from scratch, it needs to be aged, and that takes years. This is why Sagamore didn't release its first whiskey until 2016.

The whiskey that landed in the bottle is a mingling of two recipes. A sweet and creamy corn-forward rye base is layered with a 95 percent rye that adds spice and complexity. Both recipes are MGP staples that Ebersold developed himself in the 1990s. MGP shipped mature whiskey in charred barrels, which were dumped, blended, and cut to 83 proof using spring water from Sagamore Farm, then bottled at the City Garage production facility. (City Garage, a former Baltimore City DPW maintenance garage, served as Sagamore's production facility while they built their distillery.)

➤ A JEWEL BOX ON THE PIER

In 2015, the idea of upgrading Sagamore became swept up in a multibillion-dollar mixed-use community development underway in Port Covington, a neighborhood in South Baltimore. Plank vowed to construct a world-class distillery in the city he loves—and he did just that. Sagamore built

What's in the Bottle?
Sagamore Spirit Straight Rye

THE VITALS: Non-age-stated; 41.5% ABV/83 proof.

PROCESS: Sagamore's signature rye is made from two mash bills. The first is 51% rye, 43% corn, and 5% malt barley. The second is 95% rye and 5% malt. The rye mash ferments for three days in 6,500-gallon open-top fermenters, resulting in a distiller's beer at about 7.4% ABV. This wash is distilled in a 40-foot column still, then redistilled twice in a doubler. The distillate enters a gauging tank at 67.5% ABV (135 proof) and enters a #3 or #4 char barrel at 125 proof with spring water from Sagamore Farm. The whiskey matures in a barrel warehouse in its natural Maryland environment for a minimum of four years.

TASTE: Tons of baking spices like cinnamon and nutmeg carry from the nose to the palate where they are met with fruity notes like pear and cherry, accompanied by caramel and vanilla from the barrel. The finish lingers, coating the back of the throat with the creamy corn in the recipe.

a 49,000-square-foot, state-of-the-art urban waterfront distillery with a visitor's center, a tasting room, and Rye Street Tavern, a 13,000-square-foot seafood restaurant.

The distillery is equipped with a 40-foot copper column still, nine 6,500-gallon fermenting tanks, an 8,000-gallon beer well, and a 6,000-gallon mash cooker. The facility has the capacity to produce 15,000 barrels per year, about 735,000 gallons of whiskey. Sagamore's volumes are nowhere near capacity, but they gave themselves room to grow. What started as a local whiskey company is now working toward becoming a global brand and major tourist destination. Conveniently located right off of I-95, the property sits close to Fort McHenry and Under Armor's global headquarters in Locust Point.

⇥THE NEW DEAL

Building the distillery was the first step toward producing a grain-to-glass Maryland rye. The next step was sourcing local rye grain. This brought the Sagamore team to the University of Maryland, where an agricultural extension agent named Bryan Butler introduced Treacy to farmer Chris Weaver and later Ricky Bauer. Sagamore's sustainable rye program began with Bauer growing trial crops of different rye varieties to identify which was optimal for making rye in terms of flavor profile, climate, geography, and sustainability. Weaver had already been growing rye and experimenting with varietals at his Hickory Hollow farm in Carroll County, Maryland. His research was invaluable in zeroing in on an optimal strain to make Maryland rye.

The rye used by most producers, including MGP, is a rye labeled "variety non stated." VNS is a batch of rye blended in huge batches from various strains and producers. For this reason, it can't be classified as any one varietal. While this grain is typically good quality, Sagamore wanted more oversight over the quality of its main raw ingredient. That meant taking complete responsibility for the grain, starting the moment it was planted.

Convincing farmers to grow significant crops of rye is more challenging than it sounds. Rye is only subsidized as a cover crop, meaning farmers are required to destroy the crop to receive a subsidy, so there's no incentive to harvest. American farmers who do grow rye for baking and whiskey tend to do so in modest amounts. (Meanwhile, bourbon's primary grain, corn, is heavily subsidized under the Farm Bill, which promotes mass supply.) The bottom line is that planting rye is risky, and the onus was on Treacy to strike a deal that made sense for everybody.

Sagamore's first long-term deal was with Ricky Bauer at Rural Rhythm Farm in Dayton, Maryland. The parties agreed to a long-term sustainable program in which Sagamore removed risk to the farmer in a couple of different ways. First, the company paid for the seed upfront to remove the out-of-pocket expense. While typical farming contracts set price based on yield, Sagamore paid a flat, per-pound rate. This allowed the farmer to potentially triple profits on a good year, and at worst they still ended up ahead.

The next step in grain production involves drying, cleaning, and properly storing the grains. Sagamore constructed a grain mill and silo on-site at Rural Rhythm. They rent the land underneath from Bauer and oversee the storage of the grain. Treacy has finally set the course toward realizing a true grain-to-glass Maryland rye. Sagamore's first year with Weaver yielded 50,000 pounds of grains, which grew to 350,000 pounds in 2019.

⇒LOOKING AHEAD

MGP stopped producing Sagamore in 2016, the same year that the first drops of Sagamore's Maryland-distilled rye came off the still. At the time of writing, the rye is aging in a warehouse facility 20 miles from the waterfront. The Sagamore wash distilled in the Baltimore distillery is the same recipe as MPG's variety. In Treacy's view, it's the perfect representation of the round, sweet profile that Maryland rye was once known for.

The first batches of Sagamore's rye turn four years old in 2021. The release will mark the beginning of a new era for a community distillery that's become a marquise in a $5.5-billion initiative to revitalize Baltimore's historic waterfront and a boost to the local farming industry. It's a long-term investment to restore Maryland rye back to a place of glory in the whiskey universe.

Back at Sagamore Farm, the fields that inspired Kevin Plank to pursue the "rye project" were burned to the ground. The soil was turned and left dormant for 18 months. Now they are changing the nutrient patterns and the soil content. It takes a little time, but everything in the whiskey world is best done slowly. Fall 2020 marked the first planting of rye at Sagamore Farm.

THE REBIRTH OF RYE

Rye whiskey has a rich heritage in the United States that predates bourbon by 200 years. Now, thanks to these dedicated whiskey makers, the mid-Atlantic rye tradition that's been lost for an entire century is coming back.

Catoctin Creek, Purcellville, VA

ESTABLISHED: 2009

THE WHISKEYS: Roundstone Rye; Roundstone Rye Distiller's Edition; Roundstone Rye Cask Proof; Rabble Rouser Bottled-in-Bond; Braddock Oak Rye; Private Cask Sales

THE STORY: If you toured Catoctin Distillery with founder Scott Harris, you'd likely hear him tell this joke: "Twenty years of government contracting taught me a great love of whiskey." Harris was approaching 40 and burning out when he proposed the idea of building a distillery to his wife and chemical engineer, Becky. They struck a deal—Becky agreed to learn how to distill whiskey, while Scott would handle the business end. Becky Harris fell in love with distilling and crafted a rye whiskey program that employs modern equipment and traditional methods to duplicate the spirit that would have been common in the region during the time of George Washington. Meanwhile, Scott upheld his end of the bargain on the business front—Constellation Brands invested a minority stake in Catoctin in 2017, and today Catoctin Creek whiskey is in 26 states and 6 countries.

George Washington's Mount Vernon, Mount Vernon, VA

ESTABLISHED: 2001

THE WHISKEYS: George Washington's Rye Whiskey; George Washington Straight Rye Premium Whiskey; George Washington Unaged Whiskey Gift Set

THE STORY: After leaving the presidency, George Washington built a distillery at his Mount Vernon estate that produced about 11,000 gallons of rye, making it possibly the largest whiskey distillery in the new republic at the time. Two centuries later, the Distilled Spirits Council (DISCUS) and other partners funded the reconstruction of Washington's distillery, which sits alongside a waterwheel-powered gristmill, capable of grinding 5,000 to 8,000 pounds of grain a day. To christen the reconstructed distillery, legends like Jimmy Russell of Wild Turkey, Lincoln Henderson of Woodford Reserve and Angel's Envy, and Bill Samuels of Maker's Mark descended on Mount Vernon to re-create George Washington's rye whiskey, a symbolic event that put wind in the sails of the whiskey's eventual comeback. The signature rye whiskey mirrors Washington's original recipe of 60 percent rye, 35 percent corn, and 5 percent malted barley, double pot distilled and bottled unaged, just how our nation's first president used to do it.

Dad's Hat, by Mountain Laurel Spirits, Bristol, PA

ESTABLISHED: 2011

THE WHISKEYS: Pennsylvania Rye; Pennsylvania Rye Port Wine Finish; Pennsylvania Straight Rye; Pennsylvania Straight Rye Bottled-in-Bond; Pennsylvania Rye, Vermouth Finish; White Rye

THE STORY: Herman Mihalich's grandfather ran a speakeasy in the 1920s, where he sold bootleg rye made by a local family who ran stills in an abandoned coal mine just outside of town. The bar opened as a proper tavern after Prohibition's repeal, and Mihalich's dad and grandfather proudly served rye when Mihalich was growing up. When the *New York Times* predicted rye's comeback in 2006, Mihalich took notice. The trained chemical engineer was aware that there were hundreds of distilleries pre-Prohibition that had all but disappeared by the 1980s. He and partner John Cooper set about restoring rye in Pennsylvania. The secret to Dad's Hat's character is its recipe of 80 percent rye and 20 percent malt. The barley's influence is most evident in their Pennsylvania Rye, a one-year bottling aged in quarter casks, which offers a scotch-like undertone beneath the spicy rye.

Wigle Whiskey, Pittsburgh, PA

ESTABLISHED: 2011

THE WHISKEYS: Single Barrel Straight Rye; Pennsylvania Deep Cut Rye; Kilted Rye; Scotch Cask Finished Bourbon; Pennsylvania Straight Bourbon; Pennsylvania Wapsie Valley Bourbon; 4 Year Double Dutch Whiskey; City of Champions Bourbon; O'Zapft is Whiskey; Strip District Reserve 5 Year Whiskey; Roasty

THE STORY: Pittsburgh's Wigle Whiskey was named in honor of Phillip Wigle, a Pennsylvania distiller who allegedly squared off with federal tax collectors in 1794, helping spark the Whiskey Rebellion. The company is just as quirky as its name. Wigle Single Barrel Straight Rye is the cornerstone of the portfolio, a traditional Monongahela high rye recipe that's spicier than its sweeter Maryland cousin. But the whiskey program doesn't stop there. Wigle is all about innovation, collaboration, and education. They seek out new flavors by distilling endless varieties of malt, rye, and corn. Then they work with local brewers and winemakers to create funky beer and wine barrel finishes and release them as one-off bottlings.

Copper Fox, Sperryville and Williamsburg, VA

ESTABLISHED: 2005

THE WHISKEYS: American Single Malt; Copper Fox Original Rye; Peachwood; Sassy Single Malt Rye; Bourbon Mash; various barrel finish varieties

THE STORY: After landing an internship at the Bowmore Distillery in Islay, Scotland, Rick Wasmund shed his former life as an insurance agent and founded Copper Fox, a beautiful distillery and Scotch-inspired malt house and kiln in the farm village of Sperryville, Virginia, in 2005. Wasmund's love for smoky single malt and Virginia's rye tradition is evident in the Copper Fox whiskey lineup. To make Copper Fox Single Malt, a six-row barley strain developed by Virginia Tech is gently smoked with local fruitwoods before entering an ex-bourbon barrel where it's fed a steady diet of toasted wood chips to finish the whiskey. Copper Fox rye is comprised of 75 percent rye and 25 percent barley that's been gently smoked with applewood and cherrywood. Wasmund expanded in 2015 by adding a second location in nearby Williamsburg.

GLOSSARY

A

absinthe: A high-proof neutral spirit that's infused with wormwood, anise, fennel, and other botanicals. (Sorry, kids, the green fairy is just a fantasy. Absinthe does not cause hallucinations.)

age statement: An age statement on a whiskey bottle guarantees the consumer that the youngest juice in the bottle is a certain number of years old. The bottle may also contain older whiskey.

Alcohol and Tobacco Tax and Trade Bureau: The TTB regulates and polices alcohol and tobacco for the federal government, overseeing permitting, labeling, advertising compliance, and health label warnings. But what they do best is collect taxes.

alternative grains: This term is open to interpretation, but in this book, any grain in a whiskey other than corn, rye, wheat, or malt barley is an alternative grain. (Example: Koval Single Barrel Millet Whiskey.)

American Craft Spirits Association: The ACSA is a nonprofit trade group representing the US craft spirits industry.

American Distilling Institute: ADI is a for-profit trade organization founded by Bill Owens in 2003 that has been influential in kick-starting the craft distilling movement.

American single malt: According to the American Single Malt Whiskey Commission, this emerging whiskey category must be 100% barley, distilled at one distillery, made in the US, and matured in oak casks. The term has no legal definition as of 2020, but if you cheat, you will be judged.

B

barley: A cereal grain used in whiskey production; often, but not always, malted before distillation.

barrel finish: Refers to placing whiskey in a secondary cask during the maturation process. (Example: St. Augustine Port Finished Bourbon.)

Bottled-in-Bond: Rules put in place in 1897 to assure standards of quality to protect consumers. Modern craft producers create bonded whiskey to separate themselves from those blending and sourcing whiskey.

bourbon: Bourbon is all about corn. The official definition states that bourbon must be produced in the US and is required to come off the still under 80% ABV (160 proof) from a fermented mash of at least 51% corn. Bourbon is required to enter the barrel at or below 62.5% alcohol by volume (125 proof) in charred new oak barrels.

CORN BEING
PREPPED TO BECOME
BOURBON MASH

cask strength: A whiskey bottled at the proof in which it came from the barrel. A typical cask strength bourbon, for example, ranges from 110 to 135 proof.

congener: There are plenty of chemicals other than ethanol produced during fermentation that end up in whiskey, and most of these fall under the congener umbrella. Fruity esters and aldehydes like yummy vanillin, as well as nasty methanol, are a few congeners distillers contend with when crafting their whiskey.

corn whiskey: The TTB stipulates that corn whiskey is made with at least 80% corn and bottled either unaged or aged in used or non-charred new oak barrels. Corn whiskey must be distilled to no higher than 160 proof off the still, enter the barrel at less than 125 proof, and hit the bottle at a minimum of 80 proof.

F

fermentation: In whiskey making, this is the process of using yeast to convert sugar into alcohol. Wort, or mash, is placed in a fermentation tank where yeast eats the sugar and converts it to alcohol. The fermented wash is what enters the still. A typical fermentation takes 3 to 5 days.

G

grain-to-glass: A term that refers to overseeing all phases of whiskey production, from receiving the grain to bottling the final product.

K

kiln: Temperature-controlled chamber where malted grain is dried.

L

lautering: A beer term carried over to American single malt, lautering means separating the liquid from solids after fermentation before the liquid is fed into the still.

MALTED BARLEY
READY FOR KILNING

M

malting: The process of converting barley and other grain seed to malt. The seed is dampened to allow it to sprout. The sprouted seed is then dried in a kiln. This process unlocks enzymes required to convert starch to sugar for fermentation, and it unlocks flavors like chocolate and cereal.

malt whiskey: Must be comprised of no less than 51% malt barley. Otherwise, it follows bourbon rules. Malt whiskey is not synonymous with single malt, which currently has no legal definition in the United States but refers to whiskey made of 100% single malt.

mash bill: A whiskey's grain recipe.

A classic bourbon mash bill might comprise 78% corn, 17% rye, and 5% malt barley. A "high rye" mash bill example: 60% corn, 35% rye, 5% malt.

N

non-chill-filtered: It's standard to cold filter a spirit before bottling to remove residues like esters and organic compounds that cloud the whiskey when ice is added. Non-chill-filter forgoes this process, which is unnecessary if the whiskey is over 92 proof.

non-distillery products: NDP spirits are sourced and bottled off-site of the distillery.

THE TEMPERANCE MOVEMENT LED TO PROHIBITION, "THE NOBLE EXPERIMENT," FROM 1920 TO 1933.

P

peat: A fuel source from bogs in Scotland made of partially decomposed vegetable matter that's dried and burned. Peat is the source of flavor smoke for "peated" Scotch whisky. Most peated single malt is produced in the Islay region of Scotland, but American craft producers have been perfecting alternative smoked whiskeys. Corsair Triple Smoke is an example.

Prohibition: The 18th Amendment was the "Noble Experiment" that banned the sale or consumption of alcohol in the United States. The amendment was ratified in 1919 and went into effect in 1920. It was repealed by the 21st Amendment in 1933 to the great relief of a thirsty nation.

proof: A spirit's proof is double its alcohol beverage content (ABV). A 90 proof whiskey is 45% ABV. The rest is water.

R

rye whiskey: See **bourbon,** but replace corn as the primary grain with rye.

S

seed-to-glass: Seed-to-glass producers control the production of a whiskey from the farming all the way to the final product.

single barrel: A whiskey bottled from a single barrel's contents instead of whiskey made from a dumped batch.

single malt scotch: Whisky produced in Scotland, made of 100% malt barley, distilled in a pot still at one distillery, aged at least three years, and matured in an oak cask of a capacity not exceeding 700 liters (150 gallons). Small amounts of caramel coloring are permitted.

small batch: This term has no legal definition, so it is an unreliable indicator of whiskey volume and is generally categorized as marketing speak.

smoke: Refers to grains smoked with wood, peat, or other fuels before

A COLUMN STILL IS IDEAL FOR PRODUCING HIGH-PROOF ALCOHOL AND MAX VOLUME.

SORGHUM IS AN ALTERNATIVE WHISKEY GRAIN THAT IS USED IN GLUTEN-FREE BAKING.

distillation; primarily used as a flavor influencer.

sonic enhancement: This refers to blasting music to agitate whiskey and amplify maturation. Blackened American Whiskey, developed by Dave Pickerell for Metallica, is an example.

sorghum: A cereal grain used in gluten-free baking that occasionally pops up as an alternative grain whiskey.

sourcing: Purchasing whiskey from another producer and selling it under one's own label.

sour mash: Common distilling practice of adding back a portion of spillage (spent grain) from the previous mash to the next run. This lowers pH, which wards off bacteria and contributes a sour taste. Colonel E.H. Taylor is credited with developing the sour mash process.

Standards of Identity: These are rules set by a governing body regarding the parameters in which a spirit is made.

straight whiskey: Straight bourbon, rye, wheat whiskeys, etc., must first meet their prescribed requirements by the TTB. (See **bourbon**.) The spirit must also be aged in an oak container for no less than two years, and all the whiskey must come from a single state.

still, column: Invented by Aeneas Coffey in 1831, a column still is a continuous (meaning it can run as long as needed) operation that's capable of distilling clean, high-proof distillate at high volume. Most large bourbon companies use a column still.

still, hybrid: Think of a pot still (see below) with a column on top. Craft distillers love the versatility and control they have with a pot and column hybrid.

still, pot: A pot still is a traditional distillation vessel used in single malt production that's become popular in craft distilling. Unlike a column still, which is continuous, pot still whiskey is made in batches.

T

terroir: In whiskey, terroir is the influence the environment has on grain. The existence of terroir in spirits is hotly debated since the still strips so much flavor. But those who believe in it swear by it.

transparency: In the whiskey community, this term refers to the act of disclosing the truth about the origins of your product. It also refers to producers sharing methods and information with peers to improve their products and elevate the entire craft community.

triticale: A wheat and rye hybrid grain that is occasionally used in whiskey production.

W

wash: The fermented mash or wort that enters the still.

wheated bourbon: Most bourbon is distilled with a mash of corn, rye, and malt. A wheater, or wheated, bourbon replaces rye for wheat. Maker's Mark and Pappy Van Winkle are examples.

wheat whiskey: The legal definition is the same as bourbon, except wheat replaces corn as the dominant grain.

whiskey: Official TTB definition states that whiskey is a spirit distilled from fermented grain(s) at less than 95% alcohol by volume (190 proof) and "having the taste, aroma, and characteristics generally attributed to whisky and bottled at not less than 40% alcohol by volume (80 proof)."

white dog: Refers to white, or unaged, whiskey.

MOONSHINE MEANS
DIFFERENT THINGS TO
DIFFERENT FOLKS.

KINGS COUNTY DISTILLERY
moonshine
corn whiskey 200ml
40% alcohol by volume

INDEX

ACKNOWLEDGMENTS

First of all, I want to thank the talented, hard-working entrepreneurs and craftsmen featured in this book who have worked so hard to solidify the craft community. I will forever be indebted to you for living by your credo of transparency by sharing your experiences and revealing what makes your company tick and what goes into the fine whiskeys you produce: Paul Hletko (FEW Spirits); Christian Krogstad (Westward Whiskey); Rob Dietrich (Blackened/Stranahan's); Jess Graber (Stranahan's/ Tin Cup); Owen Martin (Stranahan's); Pete Lynch (WhistlePig); Ralph Erenzo (Tuthilltown Spirits); Andrew Webber (Corsair); Chip Tate (Tate & Co.); Jared Himstedt and Greg Allen (Balcones); Brian Treacy and Ryan Norwood (Sagamore); Nicole Austin (Cascade Hollow); Colin Spoelman (Kings County); Lisa Wicker (Widow Jane); Dan Garrison (Garrison Bros.); Mike Diaz (St. Augustine); Herman Mihalich (Dad's Hat); Scott and Becky Harris (Catoctin Creek); Joe Henry and Liz Henry (J. Henry & Sons); Alan Laws (Laws Whiskey House); Anna Servey (Cedar Ridge); Jason Barrett (Black Button); Eugene Marra (Cooperstown); Allen Katz (New York Distilling Company); Michael Myers (Distillery 291); Rob Masters (Family Jones); Greg Metze (Old Elk); David Weglarz (StilL 630); Scott Busch (Templeton); Phil Brandon (Rock Town); Fritz Maytag and John Dannerbeck (Anchor Distilling); Meredith Meyer Grelli (Wigle); Rick Wasmund and Cheryl Wasmund Targos (Copper Fox); Scott Blackwell (High Wire); Abby Boler (Koval); and Dennis Pogue (George Washington's).

This crew has also been instrumental in sharing their knowledge and experience and, in many cases, patience: "Ghost editor" Frank Coleman at the Distilled Spirits Council; Margie Lehrman at American Craft Spirits Association; Bill Owens at American Distilling Institute; Bill Samuels at Maker's Mark; Nick Morgan, formerly of Diageo; Beau Beckman and Madison Sevilla at Buffalo Trace; Tommy Tardie, proprietor of Fine & Rare in NYC; Tom Mooney at Westward Whiskey; Danielle Eddy; Fred Minnick; Chuck Cowdery; Wayne Curtis; Amanda Schuster; G. Clay Whitaker; Robin Robinson; Lew Bryson; Clint Lanier; Clay Risen; Leslie Sbrocco; John Torgersen (for going above and beyond); and Tony Sachs.

Next up is the also infinitely patient crew at duopress: Editor, Evan Griffith; art director, Yvonne Duran; designer, Stephanie Birdsong; copy editor, Michele Suchomel-Casey; and publisher, Mauricio Velázquez de Leon. I am honored to work with this talented team.

And, of course, the people in my life who have supported me even if they thought I was nuts for taking on this project: Andy Rae; Paul Meslin; Dan Bono; Rob Hug; Steve Kramer; Ed Dalheim; my brother, Brian McCarthy; my son, Andrew; and most importantly, my wife Al. I owe you big.

ABOUT THE AUTHOR

JOHN McCARTHY is a 25-year publishing veteran who has worked as the spirits and cocktail pundit at *Men's Health* magazine and contributed stories for *Roads & Kingdoms, Forbes, Men's Health, Maxim, JW Marriott* magazine, *Bourbon+*, and *Gear Patrol*. John is also the author of the book *The Modern Gentleman: A Guide to the Best Drinks, Food, and Accessories* and director of judging for the John Barleycorn Awards, an international spirits competition.

Cover: ffphoto/Adobe Stock
Page 6: Courtesy of Tuthilltown Spirits
Page 9: Courtesy of Stranahan's
Pages 10-13: Courtesy of Buffalo Trace Distillery
Page 17: Courtesy of Anchor Brewing Company
Page 23: Courtesy of Westward Whiskey
Page 25: Courtesy of Tuthilltown Spirits
Page 28: Courtesy of Westward Whiskey

CHAPTER 1: All images (33, 36-37, 38, 41, 43) Courtesy of Tuthilltown Spirits
Pages 46-47: Courtesy of Tuthilltown Spirits

CHAPTER 2: All images (51, 52, 54, 56) Courtesy of Westward Whiskey

CHAPTER 3: Pages 65, 69, 70, 72-73, 75 Courtesy of WhistlePig; Page 67 Iryna Mylinska/123RF

CHAPTER 4: All images (81, 83, 84, 85, 89) Courtesy of Stranahan's

CHAPTER 5: All images (95, 97, 101, 102, 103) Courtesy of FEW Spirits
Page 107: Leszek Czerwonka/123RF

CHAPTER 6: Pages 111, 113, 119, 120, 121 Courtesy of Balcones; Page 117 Courtesy of Chip Tate
Pages 122-123: Courtesy of Garrison Bros.

CHAPTER 7: Pages 127, 130, 133, 134 Photos by Jess Williams; Page 132 Photo by Andrea Behrends; Page 137 Courtesy of Corsair
Page 139: Courtesy of St. Augustine Distillery

CHAPTER 8: Pages 143, 147, 148, 149, 150, 155 Courtesy of Kings County Distillery; Page 153 Courtesy of Cascade Hollow
Pages 156-157: Courtesy of Widow Jane

CHAPTER 9: All images (161, 163, 165, 167) Courtesy of Sagamore Spirit

GLOSSARY
Page 175: Courtesy of Tuthilltown Spirits
Page 176: Photo by Jess Williams
Page 177: Illustration Currier and Ives, Public domain, via Wikimedia Commons
Page 178: Courtesy of Tuthilltown Spirits
Page 179: Marek Uliasz/123RF
Page 181: Courtesy of Kings County Distillery
Page 191 and back cover: Author photo by Ebru Yildiz
Back cover (top): Photo by Andrea Behrends

Go skinny dipping (or chunky dunking!) Feel how awesome your naked body feels surrounded by the water.

***

Stand in front of a mirror and say, "My body is an expression of divine love. Today I honor my body." Say it 20 times as you look yourself in the eye.

***

Take a sewing class and make yourself a beautiful piece of clothing that is custom made for your awesome body.

***

Before you show for a new bathing suit, find pictures of people your size wearing the type of suit you like and having fun. When you're shopping for (and maybe trying on) your new suit, keep those images in your head and think of all the fun you'll have in your new suit.

***